Advance Praise for *Addictive Ideologies*

"*Addictive Ideologies* provides an up-close look at the causes of genocide and similar atrocities from the perspective of someone whose family survived one."

-Dr. Esad Boskailo, Bosnian concentration camp survivor, author of *Wounded I Am More Awake: Finding Meaning after Terror*

"*Addictive Ideologies* gives readers a pathway to avoid authoritarianism so that atrocities don't happen on our soil."

-Phil Gordon, former mayor of Phoenix, Arizona

"My research has shown conclusively how many ordinary people can be manipulated into committing atrocities. Finding one's agency and accountability are the only real tools to avoid those dangers, and *Addictive Ideologies* is an ideal guide."

-Dr. Philip Zimbardo, American psychologist known for the 1971 Stanford prison experiment, professor emeritus at Stanford University and author of *The Lucifer Effect*

"Understanding addictive ideologies can hopefully help avoid catastrophic consequences here in today's world. This book demonstrates the risk and consequences of losing sight of who we are and who we need to be. It is a must read for everyone."

-Martin Jannol, son of a Holocaust survivor

"Judaism teaches that good and evil are an integral part of each of us. Within each person resides a *Yetzer ha Ra*, יֵצֶר הָרַע, an evil inclination, and a *Yetzer ha Tov*, יֵצֶר הַטוֹב, a good inclination. Each of us has an obligation to heed to the good inclination in the way we treat one another, even in our most intimate and innermost chambers, as described in *Addictive Ideologies*. As Jews, we must never forget that this struggle between the two inclinations, is constant and that it is our high responsibility to ensure that good always prevails over evil, in our personal lives, and in our collective world."

-Rabbi Pinchas Allouche of Congregation Beth Tefillah

ADDICTIVE IDEOLOGIES

FINDING MEANING
AND AGENCY
WHEN POLITICS
FAIL YOU

DR. EMILY
BASHAH
AND HON. PAUL
JOHNSON

LEGACY
launch pad
PUBLISHING

ISBN: 978-1-956955-49-1 (ebook)

ISBN: 978-1-956955-47-7 (paperback)

ISBN: 978-1-956955-48-4 (hardcover)

CONTENTS

In loving memory to the many people who lost their lives to genocides, holocausts, oppressive governments and addictive ideologies. And finally, to Emily's grandmother, Madeleine Bashah, for having imparted in her children and grandchildren spiritual knowledge, connection to the past and the practice of ancient traditions. She is forever alive within her family, like so many other survivors of genocide, whose only remaining purpose is to ensure that others never forget.

We dedicate this project to Ezoury Menashi Moshe Shamash, who sacrificed his life for his family; to the Bashah and Shamash families for their ability to persevere; and to the many individuals and families who suffered cultural oppression, ethnic intolerance, discrimination, human injustice, persecution or spiritual suffering. Your lives and lived experiences matter.

FOREWORD: THE DANCE
PRESENT DAY

The lights dimmed. The room's noise was at a low roar, with people laughing, eating and enjoying one another's company. Suddenly all became quiet. They turned toward the center of the room. Something they had come for was about to begin.

This was no typical American restaurant. The owner constantly walked through the room filled with people of Middle Eastern descent, making sure his customers were happy. The aroma of wonderful spices filled the air. Multiple languages were spoken, but Arabic was prevalent. Arab Americans came to this deeply ethnic establishment to feel the bond of other Arabs, to listen to Arab music and watch the cultural belly dance. And most importantly, they came to this place to feel connected. Connected to other people like them, their history and their culture. To feel connected in an American world that increasingly distrusted ethnic diversity.

Everything about the dancer who entered the room gave a sense of presence. The music was filled with drama and culture. It was music one would never hear in a typical American nightclub. The dancer's muscular body was wrapped in a beautifully beaded bedlah.

She turned away from the audience, spreading her arms and wing-like veil. She arched her back and began to roll her hips, moving her abdominal muscles in a manner that seemed impossible. Yet, it was as artistically graceful as it was sensuous. As the music intensified, she then began to spin her body at a rate that felt supersonic; even the best test pilots would become disoriented. Yet, her personality filled the space, and her smile infected even the most hardened watchers. She was in total control of every person in the room.

This was not a dance one could learn by practicing at home. Thousands of hours of training had given her the ability to move her core in ways that seemed to defy human possibility. The training was often as intensive as that of a triathlete. But from everything one could see, she made it look as if she was born with this skill.

As the dance came to a climax, her brilliant smile and effortless movement were belied by the sweat that drenched her back. The bedlah shook so vigorously that some of the tiny trinkets—so lovingly stitched on by her mother—fell to the floor. But all anyone paid attention to was the burst of art displaying itself in human form.

Young men watched her in submission as she engaged an elderly couple in dance. It was clear she had peeled back the clouds of old age and brought back another day of spring for them.

This dance would be so misunderstood in American culture, a society that long ago separated sex and fertility, that uses sex to sell anything, but has somehow lost the human art that can be tied to sexuality. This dance can be traced back to almost every ancient Mediterranean civilization. In the caves of Addaura in Sicily, drawings in the rocks almost 17,000 years ago depict a fertility dance.[1] "The Dance of the Seven Veils" is the famous dance of Salome, performed before King Herod Antipas. In Sparta, women danced for Artemis, displaying hip movements referred to as the Kordax dance. And in ancient Babylonia, a legend that began in 4,500 BCE, the goddess Ishtar covered her body with seven veiled costumes and entered the land of darkness to recover her husband. She would roll her belly, giving each layer a jewel and a veil.

The veil itself is misunderstood today. Assyrians were the first to make historical references to the veil, a sheer piece of cloth that covered the face and body, which was not meant to be oppressive but instead to create a sense of mystique. It was a symbol of social status and was unavailable for women who were sex workers or of the wrong social order. It was only for wealthy or married women. Its purpose was to hide something of greater value.

This would be altered by Samia Gamal, born in Egypt in 1924 and trained in ballet and Latin dance. She was the first to perform in high-heeled shoes on stage.[2] She soon became famous and starred in movies, including *Ali Baba and the Forty Thieves* (1954) with French comedian Fernandel and *Valley of the King* (1955) with Robert Taylor.

It would be her depiction that would turn the belly dance into something more about sexuality and less about art in American society. Gamal made the veil famous and turned it into an image of romance, sexuality and seduction.

But the veil means something very different to me. I am, in fact, that dancer. My stage name and veil disguise from the audience that the woman underneath is an Arab, and also a Jew. It hides that I have a doctorate in psychology. It does not reveal that my parents were refugees. It makes invisible the hours upon hours of training, physical exhaustion and the skills passed from one generation to the next. The veil not only conceals parts of me from the audience, but through the sheer fabric, I am able to see parts of them that would be inaccessible to a typical Jewish psychologist. Like the payment from the goddess Ishtar, it buys my way through the dimmer parts.

This dance has been a gift to me; it is as old as the Torah itself. It connects me to my Arab and Jewish ancestors. It connects me to my history. Long before the dance of Ghawazi women in Egypt made the dance famous, you can find sections of the Torah, the Talmud and the Bible that reference it. In Biblical notations in Exodus 15:20, Miriam the prophetess, the sister of Aaron, took a tambourine in her hand and all the women went out after her with tambourines, dancing. In Hebrew, the *Machol* was to whirl the body, to twirl the torso in a way that moves to contradict the limbs. In Ta'anit 4:8, it was tied to betrothal.

For me, I dance because I love it. I love the anonymity, perfecting my moves and listening to people who do not know I am Jewish, a psychologist or the daughter of refugees. I dance under a stage name that helps others identify me as an Arab. However, for me, it does not identify my politics, nor is my identity limited to the dancer or the Arab. I am also a psychologist, a mother, an American and a Jew. The observer is veiled from these other parts of who I am to create an illusion of a dancer with whom they can identify.

For me, this book is a journey through time, chronicling the lives of ordinary people in extraordinary circumstances. For the most part, these stories came to me as firsthand accounts, some through the journey of my Jewish family, tortured and escaping the tyrannical rule of Saddam Hussein, and some from my profession as a psychologist, where names and places have been changed. But nonetheless, they are real accounts of incredible events and incredible people, pointing out the important historical arcs that connect us to today.

My partner, life collaborator and co-author, Paul Johnson, and I have explored these stories together, and we have applied our thinking through my expertise in psychology and through his experiences in social trends from his time in politics. We have looked for current trends in analyzing these historic stories. We certainly have seen threads that link together the stories of refugees, people who were in concentration camps, prisoners, criminals and people who escaped from tyrannical regimes bent on ethnic cleansing.

The story could be told on its own without commentary, but we believe it is valuable to discuss those threads and trends to think about what these stories mean and how we can improve our lives and the lives of our children. It is inherently wrapped up in modern issues of identity politics, cancel culture and our rejection of those who cannot see that the values of Western democracy are far superior to the alternative.

We are focused on what we call "addictive ideologies." This book was written to help you and others understand and navigate them, and to help readers cope with the evil within themselves. It is designed to help you regain your sense of agency.

This book is separated into two halves. The first is a personal narrative and a case study of what can go wrong in a society that breaks down as a result of addictive ideologies, and the horrific consequences and atrocities that can follow. As such, it is a cautionary tale not of an ancient empire, but of recent history—more specifically, the Ba'ath Party in the 1970s. At its heart, it is the personal story of my family after the breakdown of civil society in Iraq and the eerie similarities to the politics of the US today.

The factors that cause a society to break down are complex. This story is told looking at the history and psychology of the time in all spheres, from the philosophical and ideological to the political and the personal. All of this analysis is designed to help us understand how these atrocities could happen in the United States and how we might prevent them.

The second section tries to offer a path of where to go from our current state of polarized politics. Paul and I see these giant tectonic plates moving towards one another, with people standing on the edges screaming at each other with no desire to hear what the others have to say. In the middle of those extremes is an enormous space where the majority of us live. Most of the people in the middle just want it all to stop: the rage, the resentment and the uncertainty. All we want is to just get on with our lives.

While the rule of law and our institutions are critical to our defense, this is only the case insofar as they reflect the American will. This will, or what we call agency, is the key to truly protecting our democracy. Our accountability, sense of meaning and belonging to a special ideal all relate to maintaining our agency and integrity, and to defeating tyranny.

Finally, we hope this book is at least in some part worthy of the countless victims of human injustice caused by authoritarian governments that used ideology as a means to rob the people's sense of agency in order to reach their unjust, evil dominions.

INTRODUCTION: "WHO AM I?"

PRESENT DAY

From the beginning of time, people have asked the question, "Who am I?" We ask this not only because of how we see ourselves, but because we have an expectation of how we want others to see us. We all want dignity. To gain dignity, we have to demand equality. Those people without this dignity feel invisible. And if we are made invisible, trouble lingers.

In my work as a psychologist, I help many different types of people. I have evaluated terrorists who committed terrible acts, and I have worked with immigrants stressed by the worry of forced separation from their families or returning to a place where their lives may be in imminent danger. I have worked with individuals in prison who worried about what they were missing on the outside and terrified about what they faced on the inside. I also have had hundreds of clinical clients who live ordinary lives but are burdened by extraordinary situations.

Paul has also dealt with people from all backgrounds and walks of life through his work as a mayor, a co-founder of several large corporations and a mentor to hundreds. Throughout both of our experiences, we have encountered many different people with diverse sets of issues. And in that process, we have seen patterns emerge.

I have had to try and find ways to listen to their fears and understand what their lived experiences must be without imposing my own assumptions. In witnessing their stories, I am astounded by how many people have had to confront such incredible adversity. I am amazed by how those facing lengthy sentences in the criminal justice system, people charged with terrorism, immigrants, refugees and ordinary people are all affected by very similar external conditions, and how the only sustained truth comes from within the individual. Paul, on the other hand, had to find a way to lead during times of social unrest, economic uncertainty and various sociopolitical events that bring stress and a sense of unease to us all.

One of the patterns we have both noticed is that people who feel betrayed and humiliated are often resentful, hopeless or angry as a consequence. We have noticed how that anger is often directed toward other groups—groups that they label as evil. Paul claims in his 40 years of involvement with politics that he has never heard so many people who will say they hate Democrats or hate Republicans. Groups call one another names, like Trumptards or libtards, likening them to a derogatory name for people with intellectual disabilities.

We believe one of the most important things we need as individuals is to own our agency. Paul believes that agency is never lost, just transferred; transferred to a politician or political party, to social media or the nightly news. It is lost to what we call addictive ideologies.

We also believe that each one of us is good and evil, and that down deep, we actually have instructions inside of us that help us to know the difference. Ideologies allow us to export that evil away from our own accountability and transfer it to groups we disagree with. Gone unchecked, it destroys the self.

And ignoring the signs destroys societies and can cause incredible atrocities along the way.

There are many causes of addictive ideologies—economic loss or hardship, embarrassment, loss of self-esteem or loss of identity. Ideologies can become a logical answer that absolves us of our responsibility for ourselves. Nothing makes an ideology more sticky than the feeling of invisibility.

When people feel invisible, disaster is not far away. It is not just the disadvantaged or underserved populations that feel invisible today. Americans of all economic statuses are under pressure. Paul and I are interested in the relationship that exists between the external social forces and the internal determinative ones, and in what one can do to counter these forces. Everywhere the average person looks—social marketing, books, news media and the political system—they are being warned of a coming apocalypse.

One thing is certain: alarmism is a cottage industry today. We have alarmists on every issue. Alarmists on global warming. Alarmists on the rise of a fascist right or a socialist left. We are alarmed that the curriculum in our schools might be manipulated by those who want to undermine our free market system or by those who would burn books. We are alarmed that one party might overthrow democracy or another might sabotage our economic system. We are alarmed by immigration, debt, the rise of China—and the beat goes on. Americans are filled with angst by the two parties and a 24-hour breaking news cycle telling them that we are falling apart.

Yet, there is abundant evidence that conditions for most people in the world and in the US are getting better, that America will be an unrivaled superpower for the remainder of the century, that our children will live dramatically better lives than we did and that technology will continue to create a greater standard of living for all. But regardless of the evidence, Americans are finding themselves in a new environment where information (and misinformation) is instant, where negativity is compounded through social media and where, on a daily basis, they are pounded with messages of doom. They are hearing this from politicians on both sides, which serves as an attack on the American brand.

This is not to deny that suffering exists in the world, but there is overwhelming evidence that the world is getting better on all counts. Perception, however, is often more important than reality. Some say perception *is* reality. And today, the perception pounded into people is that what they counted on in the past cannot be counted on in the future. Their lives won't be as good as their parents' lives were, and their children's lives won't be as good as theirs are. We see real effects of this pessimism in our society, and I see it daily in my work as a psychologist.

In Ray Dalio's *The Changing World Order,* he makes the case that America is on the decline and China is on the rise. He (along with other social scientists and economists) say we may be facing an era that is similar to the crash that came after 1929, a time when the world's social order was upset.[1] A period when the "-isms" were formed: communism and fascism. A time when American society itself was being tested. America First was originally a fascist movement in the US that formed right after the great crash, and America First is a major movement again today.

The year 2008 had many similarities to 1929. The Great Recession of 2008 created wealth disparity. Many Americans became angry, especially those who lost some economic ground. The sociologist Eric Hoffer wrote in his 1951 book *The True Believer* that revolution does not come from people who have a lot and want more, nor does it come from people who have little and want more—it always comes from people who had something and lost a piece of it. Our current social negativity is not about reality, where significant arguments exist that there is no better time to be alive than today. It is about the perception, exacerbated by an unprecedented alarmist era, that we may not do as well as our parents, and our children may not do as well as us.

Hoffer predicted[2] that America would not truly have to worry about a revolution until a large segment of its citizens believed either they would not do as well as their parents economically or that their children would not do as well as them. That generation who believed this loss had occurred would be the generation that would overthrow the established order. Polling shows that many people in Western democracies feel exactly this way. This feeling of discontent should be a warning sign for America, and we need to begin thinking about what we can do to counter it.

We propose that part of what our counterculture needs is to create a national effort designed around instilling optimism. This should be based on recognizing that all people of all races, identities, backgrounds and social classes must pay attention to their real economic issues. Losing ground economically leaves one with the feeling they are being left behind or forgotten. It is a feeling of invisibility. When we are invisible, we are not equal. And when we are not equal, we are without dignity. Because each of us demands dignity, when faced with feeling invisible, we act out in other ways.

Polling in the US also shows that racial minority groups are now more optimistic than white Americans.[3] But this is curious because white Americans still do significantly better economically than their minority counterparts.[4] While economically, white men still do better than other socioeconomic groups, no group in America today feels that they have lost more than white men. With the loss of blue-collar jobs, they see their economic stability taken away.[5] As social norms are changing, they feel a loss of electoral clout. Woke culture, cancel culture and political correctness all add to their feeling of invisibility.

We are seeing the effect of their loss politically and socially today. The fact is, white men are more pessimistic because they feel they are falling behind, and while some of this is based on reality, it is exacerbated by groups who benefit from its promotion.

Yet, there are real effects on real people from cancel culture and political correctness. Cancel culture has empowered a number of individuals, who through the ability to create a digital mob, appoint themselves as a moral vanguard for values that may not even come close to representing a majority of the public. This is not limited to the left, as the right will often utilize buzzwords to degrade opponents and limit speech or demand that certain books or publications be removed from libraries. In both cases, the message is often distorted, creating an unfair result for the maligned. Often, people's lives are destroyed not because of something they said, but because of what others reported that they said. But the damage is not just to the individual who is accused. It is also damaging to the accuser.

When people feel they are losing ground, it can manifest itself as anger, sorrow, despair and resentment. Generally, ideologies are thoughtful, even if sometimes destructive. They come about from elite intellectuals who string together a series of rational thoughts in a framework for how we should see issues. Thus, through ideologies, some rational thought is applied to issues. Today, the traditional conservative and liberal ideologies are being washed away. The white majority, facing losses of political clout, are now addressing issues based on how they feel as opposed to how they think. The same is happening in minority communities.

Politicians on both sides are responding to this by appealing to that anger. The politician picks a strawman, either Wall Street or immigrants, the wealthy or the poor, and tells the public that's who caused them their pain. They are intentionally creating a victim class—on both sides—stoking anger, resentment and payback. The victim is not just who they attack but who they claim to defend.

As a result, we are seeing the two political parties becoming more focused on issues of race, and those voters who are not are registering in droves as independents. In 2020, an estimated 44 percent of voters are registered as "other" or independent. Because of this, the two political parties are becoming more ideologically diluted. When 80 percent of legislative and congressional districts are gerrymandered into safe districts, we end up with most politicians only having to address one side, never facing independent voters. And thus, candidates are appealing to those diluted sentiments, resulting in greater political divisiveness.

This strategy may have short-term political gains, but from an individual standpoint, it is very damaging to the psychology of the individual. It fosters anger, frustration and the feeling of being ignored. Anger can lead to family problems, job loss, suicide or harming other people. We blame, label and harbor contempt. The damage to the system is obvious, but the effects on individuals, while not as obvious, are often catastrophic.

All of this is magnified by social media and our nightly news, which seem to take sides in the debate. And while significant studies show that our nation is not as divided as one might think,[6] it is also certain that the information we get is a message of the extremes amplified as the norm, causing people to feel they are on shaky ground.

This is the world my psychotherapy clients are trying to navigate today. I suspect that many of you reading these words are also struggling. This book is a compilation of stories from a number of people's lives, which we can hopefully learn from. We hope that my observations as a psychologist and my partner's insights into politics and sociology can help. In my practice, trends have begun to appear. Understanding the global, sociopolitical and economic impacts on the individual is key to understanding how to help people on an individual basis.

As a psychologist, I hope the powerful stories from many people's lives can help some readers find meaning, purpose and ultimately fulfillment. I will use real-life examples and lessons from the lives of terrorists, immigrants, refugees, aggrieved white males and people of color, as well as those within the criminal justice system. I will give you my parents' story, which is unique because of the massive effects on them as Jews whose families were tortured, murdered and stripped of everything they own. I hope these stories give us gratitude for where we are, a warning for where we do not want to go and recommendations for what steps we can take to avoid such calamities as individuals.

There are a few common threads that we cannot help but point out before we begin our journey. It is through these threads that I have found the ability for individuals to find success or self-destruction.

The most important common thread of our society during these divided times comes from the narrative that is created for oneself by oneself. This narrative creates the image we see ourselves through, and how others, in turn, begin to see us. It revolves around the question of, "Who am I?" And agency is all about the "I."

Understanding the narrative that others create for themselves can be difficult. Psychologists work hard to be non-judgmental and compassionate while trying to gain a deeper understanding of this narrative and someone's personal life trajectory. Paul's interest in others caused him to register as an independent so he could better understand where others were coming from. But as you move towards these more unbiased roles, you also change. Your ability to gain perspective is enhanced.

I have found that a veil often plays an important role for

Introduction: "Who Am I?"   xxv

me. I gain a very different understanding of people when I'm dancing, when I'm behaving as a regular person out in the world and when I'm a psychologist. How others identify me determines how they will respond to me. How they see me determines how they see themselves. When I dance, they see me as a fellow Arab. When they know me personally, they respond to me as female and Jewish, and this changes how they present themselves. When they see me as a psychologist, they see me as someone who is there to help them, and again, it changes what they project onto me. The same would be true if they saw me as deeply ideological or political. I find that I can hear more from them when they identify with me.

Within the identification of the self, there are two fundamental characteristics that I find are the major self-determinants. The first is whether you see yourself as having choices or constrained options. If you see yourself without options, then you are at risk of falling into the trap that you are a victim. And victims usually feel harmed, exploited and invisible. The second is whether or not you are willing to give people the benefit of the doubt, or if you objectify them to meet your needs. This becomes obvious in labeling. When you label someone, you are objectifying them, and you are simultaneously isolating yourself. In both of these cases, the reality is only what exists in the mind. These are self-created mindsets, and because you created them, you can also repair them.

As an example, you will hear stories of people who are in prison for life, certainly with constrained options, and yet, they thought through their choices and created a positive life of value. Conversely, I have provided psychotherapy and worked on other forensic cases with people who had unlimited opportunities and choices, yet through their problematic self-narratives, narrowed perspectives and self-imposed limitations, they created a very constrained path for themselves. They also further intensified their problems by labeling others, externalizing blame and refusing to take accountability for their own actions, leaving them with a loss of personal agency, power or control and making them unable to gain from the skills of others different than them. I would like to add a qualifier here —while I am making some generalizations in order to offer some psychological insights that my clients have taught me through their success, growth and transformation, these generalizations do not necessarily apply to everyone. There are cases, such as severe psychopathology, intellectual disabilities, psychotic disturbances and serious conditions that are truly limiting. We all have a growth potential curve, and that may be different for each individual.

We will spend significant time talking about these two concepts, one through the victim triangle and the other focused on how objectifying people places us in a box. For those who prefer to read the shortened version, I will list the advice that I give over and over to clients. This is attached in the back as part of the appendix. However, all this advice fits back into the self-narrative—issues revolving around choices versus limited options, and giving people the benefit of the doubt versus placing them into categories.

Finally, the concept of agency plays an important role in this book. Traditionally, agency refers to the human capacity to influence one's functioning and the course of events through one's actions. Agency is determined by: insight, empowerment, intentionality, forethought, self-regulation and self-reflection. You may not be able to control your destiny but you can control your fate. Controlling your fate is determined by you owning your agency.

In this book, we will focus on how you can lose your agency and how you can get it back—and how addictive ideologies can steal agency from you, even when you think an ideology is just normal political thought. Owning your agency is key to having a meaningful life, to creating, innovating, rationalizing and thinking. To own your agency, you must be able to use the neocortex portion of the brain where you can access rational thoughts, creativity, innovation and optimism. You can lose your sense of agency through fear, despair and depression. These can be affected by others who manipulate you and your negative bias in order to steal your agency.

We will talk about the loss of agency through addictive ideologies. We will show the stories we know personally where these addictive ideologies have destroyed lives and societies. We will argue that through our current politics, cancel culture, political correctives and nationalism, these addictions are present in today's society. But most importantly, we hope to illuminate you on the Seven Ideals of Citizenship necessary to own your agency. These include:

1. Know the Truth
2. Your Uniqueness Entitles You the Right to Begin Anew
3. Meaning Over Happiness
4. Leverage Yourself
5. Find Power in Love and Connection
6. We, Not Me
7. Believe in You, Believe In Us and Act With That Belief

As a disclosure, Paul and I differ significantly on political issues. However, where Paul and I find agreement is around the power of the individual. From the Stoics to the founders of our country, Western society has been based on the dignity of the human spirit that is in each one of us. That while we may not all be equal, we expect the government to treat us equally. We see ideologies as generally harmful to the individual. We see benefits from the left and the right, and we see the extreme factions of both as extremely dangerous to the individual and to American society. We believe in modernism and reject most aspects of postmodernism. We love rational thought and believe in science. We believe that most of the problems mankind faces can be solved by mankind.

This story is designed to be told through the stories of others, and no story has had a bigger effect on my life than that of my parents who were refugees from Iraq. Their families were persecuted, tortured and murdered by Saddam Hussein. Many stories are spread throughout this book—but this is where we will start.

PART I

ADDICTIVE IDEOLOGIES

1

THE HANGINGS
JANUARY 27, 1969—TAHRIR SQUARE, IRAQ

لا تُشرق الشمس في منتصف الليل، ولكن في قمة اليأس ينبت الأمل

"The sun does not rise in the middle of the night,
yet at the center of despair rises hope."

-Gibran Khalil Gibran

A cold crisp air filled his lungs. As he walked towards the scaffold, his heart began to beat so hard that he could feel it in his throat. The stones stuck to his bare feet, and they hurt as he walked up the wooden stairs. The sign around his neck stated he was a Jew and told of the crime he had been accused of days before on a televised mock trial. He was just a 17-year-old boy.

His desperate eyes searched the angry crowds, looking for someone who might come to save him. He had done all that his captors had told him. He had told the court he was older so they could hold his trial. He knew he was not a spy for anyone.

He believed that in the end, his innocence should matter. He knew someone had to stop this madness. But now, all he could do was cry.

The Arab crowd at Liberation Square was large, and they were at a fever pitch. People spat on the men walking up to the gallows. They threw rocks at them and hit their legs with sticks.[1] The young boy saw the other men in front of him that had been accused of similar crimes. He watched them as they began to resist or fall apart in the last few seconds of their lives.

He felt the sack being pulled down over his face. He felt the heat of his breath, the beating of his heart. As the noose was lifted around his neck, terror shivered through his body, releasing any control he had over his bodily functions. The man began to tighten the rope under the boy's chin. He gasped for air. He begged God to save him.[2]

Across Liberation Park, another Jewish boy, 19-year-old Joseph Bashah, was riding his bike home. He could hear the commotion, the people cheering and shouting insults. As he looked across the park, he saw the sacks over the heads of the condemned men and boys on the gallows. Panic rose in his chest. He knew this was related to the trial of Jews. This was why everyone he knew was so terrified.

That 19-year-old boy was my father.

These hangings are not just about the cruelty of Saddam Hussein. The larger story is about numerous people on all sides whose identity politics, addictive ideologies and the loss of personal agency created a human catastrophe.

In his book *Identity*,[3] Francis Fukuyama, an American political scientist and economist, writes about how identity affects Western democracy. He uses the Greek theory of *thumos* and connects it to the modern concepts of identity politics. From Ancient Greece, Thumos indicates a physical association with breath or blood and is also used to express the human desire for recognition. It's related to how an individual wants to be recognized by their government, and it asks not only the question of who am I, but it creates a connection to dignity. It was the earliest recorded concept that focused on defining identity.

However, this thumos in Greece only applied to a special class. Much later, Christian theologian Martin Luther would tie this inner dignity to a direct relationship with God, which bypassed the church and created the Reformation. However, for Luther, this was strictly a binary decision, to accept or reject God on a personal basis. Later, Swiss-born philosopher Jean-Jacques Rousseau would inspire the French Revolution and even the American Constitution through documents like his *Social Contract*, that instilled the entitlement of the basic rights to all men. He expanded the power of the inner individual to secular concepts.

As these concepts played out in the American Revolution and our Constitution, we first granted property rights to white men only. Over time, this expanded to Black men, then women, then additional marginalized groups. Some still fight for this right to this day. The inner self demands dignity. And one can only get dignity with equality.

This is the basis of Western democracy, in which the individual's rights are valued over the collective. Individuals then demand dignity and equality from the government. And when it is denied, there is discontent.

When we suffer an individual setback, we must grapple with how it happened. When a natural disaster occurs, it's almost easier on the social order because you can easily see what caused our problem. But when the state or the invisible hand of a free market is the cause of loss, discontent or failure, knowing who to blame is much more difficult.

In 2008, the housing bubble caused the Great Recession. Low interest rates and lack of regulation allowed people to purchase multiple homes or qualify for loans well above their income level. There was something called a Liar Loan, where borrowers constructed false income to qualify for a loan. Eventually, the truth had to come out, and as those who could not afford their new debt began to default (more than six million), our economic system began to crumble.

Certainly, lending standards, government action and inaction, and banks and lenders were culpable. We blamed Wall Street not Main Street, when actually we all played a role. More importantly, fixing these problems would require sacrifice from everyone.

So when the economy faltered, the ideologies on both sides began to foment. Blame was placed on bankers, the rich, immigrants and so on. And new ideologies began to form out of the old. The far-right and the far-left became more emboldened. Then all ideologies began to blame one another for additional societal problems as they created more electoral success. Through this blaming, we were able to export our own culpability and place it on others.

We do not believe that this problem is nearly big enough to topple America itself or destroy the institutions that protect our freedoms. But go back to the hangings. They are an example of the effects of economic issues on societies where the institutions are not as strong as ours. In understanding those events where civility broke down, we can understand how important it is to protect the institutions of freedom in American society. We consider the agency of the individual to be the greatest institution of freedom we must protect.

Look around us today. It is not hard to see that once the demand for equity is resolved, there is a short line to a demand for superiority. This has become the narrative in the current battle of extremes in the US. White nationalism, woke culture, political correctness and cancel culture are topics spoken about daily on our nightly networks. These individualistic ideologies do not want equality. They want superiority, and the media stokes division.

The news media is sacrificing its objectivity and the soul of our country for votes and viewership. There is no room to celebrate, only to criticize. Our screens have become an inexhaustible stream of pessimism, beating us down daily into submission, partisanship and savior-worship.

In this environment, where can optimism and progress live? We've been convinced that the ground is constantly shaking and the sky is on the brink of collapse. Who can take pride in a country that's constantly painted as flawed and increasingly vulnerable? In this environment, we witness the effect of addictive ideologies. We are seeing the negative effects of a loss of national identity. And inevitably, we are seeing many people lose their sense of agency.

Certainly, having a national identity can be a good thing. Without it, our citizens no longer tie their identity to pride in being Americans. Then, support for the institutions breaks down. Corruption, loss of faith and finally, civil war become possible. With national identity, it is easier to implement a social safety net as the public supports people who they see as part of their communal family.

Most importantly, a national identity is important to preserving democracy itself. Democracy demands an incredible amount of compromise. And that compromise can only happen when people feel it serves a greater purpose. Without that greater purpose, without compromise, the threads of democracy begin to unravel.

However, if national identity becomes ethnically based, if it is aggressive and disregards compromise, it can become increasingly destructive. From such environments have come the big genocides. This was clearly an issue in Iraq during the hangings. Nationalism and religion overpowered the system.

White nationalism has always been an issue in the US. We fear that the fires of white nationalism are currently being stoked, unwittingly or wittingly, as much by the left as the right.

This much is certain: in an environment of woke culture, cancel culture and political correctness, we have stifled conversation.

Certainly, thinking needs to evolve on the issues of human rights and equal rights. However, when you bully people or intimidate them to be quiet, you make them invisible. They don't go away, they just simmer. One day, someone comes along and speaks to the invisible, defends them, and it turns into a boil. After he or she defends them, recognizes them and makes them feel seen, they will follow that person regardless of if they lie, cheat, steal or say incendiary things—or even defraud elections.

So if a common national identity is essential to human progress, when is identity politics a problem? We believe it is when the identity is tied to one's negative bias. When the information used to create one's identity is based on fear, anger, resentment and hatred. Once the reptilian part of the brain is engaged in these emotions, one loses the ability to think rationally, optimistically and creatively, and so one loses a sense of agency.

This can become obvious when an individual uses their identity to label others. Trumptards, libtards, white privilege, feminazi and other labels are used by the opposing sides today. When we label others, we do extreme damage to ourselves. We isolate ourselves and we deny ourselves the gifts of other people who are not like us.

Identity politics is a problem when it begins to suppress the rights of others, specifically their freedom of speech. White nationalism tries to pass on cultural pride by oppressing others. The other side looks to oppress who they see as the oppressor. They tie this to capitalism without regard for the wide ranging benefits it has provided or the significant oppression that can come from socialism.

Both the right and the left have moved in the direction of identity politics, and in the process, have arguably lost their sense of agency. Politicians, responding to the incentives created by a partisan system where very few vote in the primaries, intentionally try to manipulate the emotions of their base. These politicians live in districts so gerrymandered that those elected in the primary face no real opposition in the general.

According to statistics, approximately 70 percent of voting-age Americans are registered. If 35 percent are represented in either party, that results in approximately 24 percent (35 percent of 70 percent) of the voters who can vote in either primary. But it becomes more insidious when you realize that only 35 percent of those voters show up in the primary. This results in less than ten percent of the potential voters taking part in selecting either the Democratic or Republican candidates. In Congress, because of gerrymandering, 400 out of 435 districts are safe from opposition. This results in less than ten percent making a choice for the other 90 percent of the district. These politicians have extreme incentives to worsen the problem.

Certainly, significant evidence exists that the extreme nationalistic right is a danger to the country. But one of the big challenges today with identity politics is the politics of the left, which inflames the rise of identity politics on the right. Through woke culture, cancel culture and political correctness, there are many voters on the right who feel they are becoming invisible.

As deindustrialization took place, especially in areas like the Rust Belt, the voters who suffered the economic loss looked for who to blame. What they saw and heard were comments they felt were derogatory by those they considered to be elites. Comments like "redneck," "white trash" or "privileged white man" made the problems worse. And the type of work done by blue-collar workers seemed to be not only reduced but diminished as a legitimate job. Political correctness made them feel invisible. And they sat quietly waiting for a leader.

All of this was happening in a general economic time when jobs were expanding. This is not to defend the many actions that have been unfair to minorities. It is only to recognize that if we do not understand and empathize with both sides, we are bound to fail. In many parts of the country, steel mills were closed, coal mines closed, factories were shut down and the workers inside these plants were displaced, leaving them and their communities in desperate positions. Pensions were changed, dramatically affecting workers' retirements. White male workers were affected disproportionately. We believe that all people are valuable and worth saving. But even more importantly, both sides are being intentionally inflamed by the 10 percent of the people who do not like the societies that Western democracy has created, and so the inequities are being exaggerated.

Imagine for a moment the Arab citizen in the square, screaming condemnations at the nine young men who were wrongfully accused. The two Jewish boys who were crying, begging for their lives. Years later, when these Arab citizens remember the frenzy, remember how they too were caught up in the moment, filled with rage, unable to see their own inhumanity, I ponder how they might see themselves today.

When taunting, spitting or abusing the men who marched to the gallows, the justification was "Jews were evil." In looking back, they might see that it was wrong to further aggrieve those condemned men but justify it by shifting blame to the Ba'ath party, Hussein, religious leaders, conspiracy groups, the media or maybe even the collective for spreading false information.

In 2020, the people who threw park benches into Capitol windows, overran barricades and beat a police officer to death also justified their actions. They justified the gallows outside, the men defecating on the hallowed floor where the Republic sends its representatives. They justified all of this based on their hatred for the elite, the media and maybe democracy itself.

In court, some of them have shifted the blame to Trump, the media, groups like QAnon or society itself. However, in an individualistic society, we can't blame the collective. In the US, the individual is in an exalted position, and thus individuals must also be accountable for their actions. Freedom and accountability are tied. As of this writing, 896 people have been charged with crimes related to the Capitol riots, and a good number have received serious time.

But genocides do not grow in a vacuum. Tyranny doesn't happen with only 896 bad guys. In the hangings in Iraq, a large group of people in the square gave away their agency to an ideology. They used that ideology to transfer the potential evil inside of themselves to the Jews who were on the gallows for nothing more than being Jews. They gave up their agency and did not hold themselves accountable.

This does not absolve the politicians who were part of the same party but turned a blind eye. Or who defended the hangings by saying it was being blown out of proportion. Or who revealed their lack of courage by justifying the killings based on what the other party was doing. It is certain that many Iraqi officials understood that what was happening to Jews was wrong, but they justified their actions based upon the personal benefit of staying in power. This same justification exists in Washington today—look no further than the January 6th insurrection.

In Washington, this use of moral equivalence by Republicans who know better does not absolve the Democrats. They too should be held accountable for using the Capitol riots to fan the flames of division in this country. Certainly, it is important to prosecute people guilty of crimes, but the Democratic

Party ran ads to help election deniers win Republican primaries because they believed it would make it easier for the Democrat to win in the general election. This tells us they are not that different from Republicans who look the other way and risk the Republic so they can stay in power.

Before we put a pox on them both, what about us? What about you and me? One of the first steps of owning your agency is being accountable for yourself. Have you ever used a derogatory term to label people who think differently than you? Have you ever called someone a redneck, Trumptard, libtard, a fascist or a socialist?

If you're a Democrat, have you rolled your eyes at someone who said something wrong because they didn't have a high school diploma? Did you ever ask someone, "Where did you get that information from, Fox News?" as if that made their opinion less valuable? Have you made a snide comment on social media? Have you ever looked down on the intelligence of someone simply because they did not have your educational background? If any of these things are true but you still believe that only Republicans are responsible, then your loss of agency is much greater than you might believe.

The people who stormed the Capitol believed they were right. They absolved themselves by saying the election was fraudulent, by seeing Trump as ordained or by seeing Trump's opponents as evil. This was based on information they received from Trump, the party, right-wing media and conspiracy groups. But before thinking that the big lie is only a possibility on the right, this is ironically similar to the cancel culture movement that quite often attacks college professors, sometimes for things they said and sometimes for things they didn't say, all based on information from others.

The ideologies of the right and the left want true believers. They hope to terrify the supporters of the other side. They hope to engage the reptilian part of your brain so you are unable to utilize the neocortex where rational thought exists. They are selling opium, and they are looking to make you addicted. Addicted to their news station, their party, their candidate or their social media site. They are intentionally creating addictive ideologies designed to take your sense of agency from you.

The high tensions in America are a warning sign not to take our individual liberties for granted. We will not recover by attacking, insulting or alienating people with whom we disagree, by the media stoking the flames or by politicians putting their own power above the health of the Republic. We will only get out of this by listening, compromising and empathizing with people we do not agree with. We will only recover by finding gratitude for all we have and from finding optimism about our future.

Iraq, Nazi Germany, Cambodia, Rwanda and other places where genocides occurred lacked enough citizens who knew the truth, who had a sense of meaning, who were accountable for themselves and willing to listen to people they didn't agree with. If they had enough of these types of citizens, those genocides would never have taken place. We are still a long way away from losing our Republic, but the sign posts are up, and they are telling us: take notice.

It's easy to see the evil in the crowd at the hanging or in the Capitol riots, in the Republicans or Democrats in office or the media and conspiracy theory groups. The harder work, the work that provides real value, is taking account of ourselves. But this work creates change beyond anything you might imagine.

In taking responsibility for ourselves, we can find meaning. We can find the benefits of people who don't think exactly like we do. We can find growth, love and purpose. We can find the truth. If we break our addiction to ideologies and regain our agency from those who would use it for their own means and self-aggrandizement, we can find the great optimism that allows us to create, innovate and find opportunities that are unavailable in our addiction.

We fix society one person at a time, and it starts by taking account of ourselves. I can create a better me. You can create a better you. And through creating a better me and a better you, we will create a better us.

2

THE PSYCHOLOGY OF TERRORISM
MAY 2021—A MAXIMUM SECURITY US FEDERAL DETENTION FACILITY

I stood outside the US Federal Detention Facility, on land under the control of the United States government. The heat outside was sweltering and it wasn't much better inside. The asphalt parking lot made the walkway into the prison feel like going through Hell's inferno. As I walked to the entryway, I could hear the hissing sound of unidentified insects in the scant brush around the building.

Everywhere I looked, it was clear this was a maximum security facility. Cameras were everywhere. There was barbed wire on the fencing. The building was devoid of any architectural features that signaled the facility had any concern about who was inside. As I entered the front door, I was greeted by armed men. The scowls on their faces told me they were serious.

I was there to evaluate a man I will call Omar who had been accused of heinous crimes against the United States. He was Islamic, an Arab Iraqi with a large frame, a light-skinned complexion, thick, jet-black hair and a long wiry beard. The reasons for my evaluation remain confidential and are not disclosed in this publication.

I had been appointed to this case because of my Iraqi

heritage and my ability to speak Arabic. My role was to evaluate Omar, an Iraqi man who only spoke Arabic and who everyone believed to be very dangerous—a man who, himself, trusted no one. Yet, my role was to get him to trust me so we could help move his hearing forward.

In the lobby, I went through the first level of security. There was an extensive check on my credentials. Then I was led into a secure set of hallways where at each door, the guard spoke only to a mic and the cameras. After I answered the questions, I waited until I heard a loud beep echo through the hall. The door clicked open permitting me to pass. This led me to another set of halls, each with the same security protocol. Presumably this was not designed to keep me out, but to keep the detainees from escaping.

After clearing the hallways, we took an elevator down several floors to a basement. Before I entered the elevator, I encountered three armed guards who were escorting another detainee. When the elevator door opened up, they took the inmate in first and had him face the wall. They told him not to turn around and demanded he not look at us. Then, they turned to me with very serious looks on their faces and told me to get into the elevator and stand on the other side. I wondered why I couldn't just wait until it was empty, but the guard was issuing a directive, not an invitation. I entered.

The smell of the inmate hit me right in the face. As I walked into the elevator, I had to control my gag reflexes at the strong ammonia odor of urine mixed with the stench of fecal matter. The heat that filled that little room combined with the smell made me nauseous.

When the elevator reached its destination, the door opened and we entered a detention room. The guards let us out first. As we stepped onto the new floor, I had that nauseous feeling all over again.

On this floor, where I would meet Omar, the number of

inmates was limited to two; the cells were stacked on one another, with a guard stationed nearby to watch the detainees. Omar was in the first row of cells. He refused to talk with me if the guards were nearby, so I went to his cell alone.

I was dressed in black slacks, a striped button-down collared shirt and a black blazer. My thick, curly hair was tied back in a low ponytail. I was dressed conservatively with no makeup or jewelry. While making these attempts to not appear physically attractive, suppressing my sexuality, I knew I was still violating Omar's expectations of a woman sharing his cultural heritage.

The front of his cell was thick plexiglass. This allowed me to see everything inside his room. However, it allowed nothing to pass back and forth, not even sound. There was a small trap door where food could be given to him. This door was not only necessary for food, but the door being open was the only way to hear what was on the other side. The rooms were designed so that an inmate in one room could not hear or speak to another.

Before I left the guards, one asked me if I wanted a spit mask to be placed on Omar's face. I knew this would destroy any confidence he might have in me, so my answer was no. I second-guessed myself when I recalled from the records that Omar had been smearing fecal matter on the walls and urinating on the food. But I held to my decision. The goal was to create a rapport with Omar in order to evaluate him.

I started the conversation: *"Salaam Alaikum."* This Arabic greeting meaning "peace be unto you" is the standard saluta-tion among members of the Nation of Islam. He emphatically replied back with a curious smile: *"Wa-Alaikum-Salaam!"*

I knew it was the Islamic holy time of Eid al-Adha, the cele-bration of Ibrahim (Abraham)'s willingness to sacrifice his son for Allah. In many countries, as Muslims prepare to observe Eid al-Adha, they fast the day before the Eid starts, marking what is known as the day of Arafat, one of the holiest days on the Islamic calendar. I acknowledged the Eid and inquired if he had been fasting. He replied that he attempted as best as he could given the circumstances of being incarcerated.

Growing up, Arabic was the main language of my home. During my time in Canada, I also became fluent in French. And with Jewish parents, I was also familiar with Hebrew and Jewish traditions. Because I learned Arabic from my parents, I have a detectable Iraqi dialect, which piqued Omar's interest. He began to inquire about my background.

Omar might have been deemed an endangerment to the United States—and here in this facility, he was often portrayed as an animal—but I was impressed that he displayed his Arab manners with me. Culturally, it would have been rude for Omar to ask me directly about my religion, which is more viewed as one's tribal affiliation and a quick detector of whether a person belongs to the friend or foe category. So he inquired into the region my parents were from, hoping to extract some information to identify me while maintaining respect and being cordial. The area my family was from was affluent, making him suspect even less that my grandfather Ezoury was Jewish. Even my name, Bashah, does not appear to most Iraqis as a Jewish name. Had Omar learned that I was Jewish, it would have likely impaired the rapport. Our conversation quickly shifted to a discussion of our favorite Arabic foods and delicacies.

I asked Omar if I could have the guards place us in a confidential room together, but he refused to leave his cell. Omar wanted me to submit dates by mail so he could consider the request and respond formally. I understood that this was an expression of self-determination in a place that removes the free will of a person. This was his way of exercising choice and some semblance of personal power, so I politely obliged.

All of us have a construct—an invisible moral and ethical architecture—for how we see society. That construct is usually determined by the government and institutions that govern us as well as the religion—or lack of religion—with which we associate ourselves.

In the United States, we live under a construct based on a social contract, one that puts the individual at the center of our American political faith. This faith can be traced to the great philosophy of antiquity, Stoicism. The Greek Stoics of antiquity believed that all people were manifestations of one universal spirit. Epictetus said, "Each human is primarily a citizen of his own commonwealth."

Stoics were the first in recorded history to promote the philosophy that individuals had universal rights and unalienable rights. These rights came because of an inner *thumos*, similar to a spirit—something inside of us that was unique. Kings have long promoted the idea that the natural order was God, the King and then the Law. It was the job of the King to interpret and enforce the desire of God. The Stoics told us that the individual had rights even over a king.

The Romans would continue this, albeit with a greater balance between the individual and the collective through a senate and a forum. Again, they promoted the idea of the powers within each of us as individuals. The Magna Carta and later, Martin Luther, would advance these same ideas.

Thus, the cornerstone of our American Republic is the rule of law, focused on the rights of the individual and collective through our social contract. The social contract of the American system is based on the fundamental idea that man is good and people can govern themselves. No man is above the law, and thus, the law is designed for all men through these unalienable rights. It is the function of that law to assure the protection of the individual.

While Christian-Judeo views dominate American society, these exist under the rules of the social contract. It is not a social contract that exists under the Christian-Judeo law. With the individual being at the center, the individual can choose to take part in any religion. But for Omar, his views were very different.

Omar's construct was based in Islam. Omar was, by definition, an Islamic extremist who believed that Islam had been corrupted by the modern world. Understanding his construct was key to understanding his worldview. But this worldview came from an ideology that he had long before become addicted to. One that had dramatically done great harm not only to others, but had destroyed his life and the life of his family. In addition, understanding his construct was essential to understanding if he was competent to meaningfully engage in legal proceedings, to have a factual and rational understanding of the legal system, his rights and his ability to assist counsel in his own defense.

The prophet Muhammad was born in Mecca, Saudi Arabia in 570 AD. Muslims believe he was the final prophet sent by God to reveal their faith to mankind. Islam teaches that the angel Gabriel visited Muhammad in 610 AD in a cave and ordered Muhammad to recite the words of Allah. Muhammad began preaching around 613, and in 622, Muhammad traveled from Mecca to Medina in what became known as the Hijra. This marks the beginning of the Islamic calendar.

In 629, Muhammad returned and conquered Mecca, dying in 632. The first four caliphs that proceeded him conquered large regions of the current Middle East. This would include what is now Iraq, Iran, Palestine and Syria. It eventually spread across Europe, Africa and Asia, lasting for centuries, and later evolved into the Ottoman Empire, which lasted from 1517 to

1917. This was the period of rule in which my maternal grandfather, Ezoury, grew up.

Islam is divided into multiple sects. The debate about Muhammad's replacement came from the major sects of Shia and Sunni. The first two caliphs to succeed Muhammad were his father-in-laws, Abu Bakr and Caliph Umar. The third was his son-in-law, Uthman. The Sunnis, who make up 90 percent of all Muslims, see these three as legitimate caliphs. Shiite Muslims see them as illegitimate. They believe the first caliph was Ali, Muhammad's son-in-law, who succeeded these three. Shiites are a minority in Islam but make up substantial portions of Iran, Iraq and Syria.

In 1979, the Islamic Revolution happened in Iran, when the Shah of Iran was overthrown. This is considered by most scholars as the rise of Islamic fundamentalism over traditional Islam, although some debate exists among those who consider the Khawarij sect in the 7th century and Saudi Arabia's Wahhabism to be fundamentalist, a movement that began in the 18th century.

Major differences in fundamentalism include only associating with Muslims, strict conformity to Sharia law without modern adaptations and a belief that women should not be educated or be able to participate in social, political and economic life. The Islamic fundamentalist groups today have mushroomed, including Al-Qaeda, Boko Haram, the Taliban, Egyptian Islamic Jihad, Hamas, Harkat-ul-Mujahideen, Indian Mujahideen, the Islamic State of Iraq and Tehrik-i-Taliban Pakistan, among a number of others.

It is important to point out that while a large number of radical Islamic organizations exist, the overwhelming majority of Muslims do not associate with these organizations, even in the countries where the organizations are based. Muslims are frequent victims of the violence of these organizations, and recent polling has found that in countries that are comprised of a Muslim majority, a vast number of citizens have very negative views of this fundamentalism.

Omar was part of the Muslim minority that was associated with the radical version of Islam. In his mental construct, the individual was not at the center of his philosophy, but instead, salvation was at the center. By constructing a society based on Sharia law, he believed that the ends could justify the means, regardless of what the means did to innocent individuals.

Constructs help create justifications for our individual actions. Omar's indoctrination into a radical philosophy could still leave him competent to engage in legal proceedings.

How one individual treats another, in my experience, in all societies and in all constructs, matters. Maiming or murdering someone, raping someone and physical or psychological torture are all violations of Western democratic mores. However, when the individual is not at the center of someone's construct, it is easier to justify these acts if they somehow benefit the collective.

A danger for all individuals and all societies is the lack of accountability. When an individual harms someone, it is human nature to create a justification for why it was acceptable. Instead of being accountable and recognizing one's own culpability and the potential for evil inside of themselves, they create justifications for the wrongful act. Those justifications are usually labels: the injured was an infidel, a heretic, a liberal, a woman, a Nazi or a right-winger. Those labels give the aggressor a justification for the offense. They also give the aggressor a false reality and skewed perception. These justifications can become the pretense for greater wrongdoing and grave harm to humanity.

In our society, labeling is usually our way to create a justification for our own actions, even if it is limited to belittling another person. When we do this, we put ourselves into a separate category that we view as somehow superior. As someone who provides psychological treatment, unless the aggressor learns to view the harmed as an individual instead of an object, my chances of success at helping the aggressor is very low. Radical organizations provide such strong indoctrination by using labeling that it creates a justification for horrific forms of violence such that it may become impossible for the aggressor to experience remorse for their crimes.

One can have a radical ideology that would lead them to committing heinous crimes but still be cognizant enough to be responsible for their decisions. For an individual to be deemed as not competent to engage in legal proceedings, for instance, they would need to have a psychotic disorder, manic episode or a delusional belief system. Buying into a radical doctrine is not the same as having a delusional belief system and is therefore insufficient in itself to be the causal condition of one's incompetence. For example, some Americans who joined the memberships and ideologies of QAnon or the Proud Boys became part of the Capitol insurgency. These beliefs and behaviors would be considered a marked deviation from social norms and antisocial or aberrant by nature, but not delusional en masse. Their subculture has formed around a radical ideology that perpetuates a justification for and condones such extremist acts.

When I returned to the detention center a few weeks later, I met Omar in a confidential room. He was chained at the wrists, waist and feet. The chain at his back was then attached to the floor. His movement was entirely restricted. Two guards remained standing behind the closed door.

I knew the crimes Omar had been involved with were significant and, in forensic settings, this was considered a high-profile case. He had harmed a great many people. I knew that while he did not suspect that I was Jewish, he still considered me to be below his worthiness for different reasons—I am an American, a woman, and in his mind, an infidel. I represented someone who did not adhere to his religious standards, faith and ideology, and who opposed his value system. He knew that the orthodoxy of his faith was shared by very few, and certainly not by an American woman, regardless of whether or not he viewed her as Muslim. For him, killing infidels was justified by the Jihad. Knowing this does not condone the crime and malicious acts of violence against humanity, but it helps to understand the psychology of perpetrators of such forms of violence. More importantly, if we can pinpoint the consistent factor that differentiates these perpetrators from others, then we can better target prevention efforts for those who may fall prey to indoctrination into radicalized ideologies. I worked hard to remain objective and ultimately to not objectify him in turn.

For hours, we discussed Omar's life, where he had come from and his lived experiences. He described the context and circumstances under which he grew up. He was an oppressed minority and suffered torture and political persecution. He was not reared with a radical version of Islam, but the persecution of his tribe as a Shia Muslim, and the fear of speaking out on his beliefs, made him feel invisible.

Like Omar, my mother and father had been victims of Saddam Hussein's torturous regime. Certainly, Omar had family members like my grandfather, Ezoury, who was tortured and killed at the hands of Saddam's Ba'ath Party. Seeing Omar from this standpoint helped me to not objectify him. Regardless of our pasts, we were just two people having a conversation. This was not to justify Omar's actions, but to simply learn about him, his worldviews and constructs so I could communicate with him.

What drives an individual towards certain behavior can help you evaluate why a society moves in a certain direction.

Answering major world problems will come in large part from trying to understand people we do not agree with, people we may not even like. Knowing their narrative and listening to their pains is key to resolving our differences. Responding to the divisions in the United States will require us to identify the effects of ideology and to give our citizens the power to restore their own agency.

As mentioned earlier, the sociologist Eric Hoffer studied mass movements and revolutions. I agree with Hoffer that pride can be a substitute for the loss of self-respect. Nationalism is a form of pride. When the loss of self-respect is a societal issue, when it affects the masses, nationalism is at the door.

When government policies, economic failure or historical incidences make it difficult for an individual to gain self-respect, nationalism becomes more extreme. Hoffer, in *The True Believer*, said:

> Faith in a holy cause is to a considerable extent a substitute for the lost faith in ourselves. . . .The less justified a man is in claiming excellence for his own self, the more ready he is to claim all excellence for his nation, his religion, his race or his holy cause.

Relatedly, the Pulitzer Prize-winning philosopher historians Will and Ariel Durant said, "When our economy of freedom fails us at length, then the road to dictatorship will be open to any man who can persuasively promise economic freedom to all."

The Germans' loss in World War II and the failure of the German currency created a fervor in the German people. This resulted in nationalism. The Nazi Party was the National Socialist Party that combined nationalism and socialism. Hitler's speeches were filled with how great the German people were and how immigrants had destroyed Germany. Individual self-esteem in Germany was destroyed by the loss of wealth, and this was replaced by false national pride.

Omar was victimized as a Shia by the Sunni Ba'ath Party. His family, financial stability and eventually his self-esteem were stolen from him by the brutal actions of the Ba'ath Party. Omar created a substitute for his loss of self-esteem and visibility through a religious order, an extreme sect of the Shia.

All Shias believe the first Caliphate was Ali. Ali was from the same clan as Muhammad. But the radical Islamic sect that Omar took part in believed that a messianic figure, the Mahdi, would return and apply strict Islamic law. He would unite the Islamic world. He would be the return of a Caliphate. Most scholars say there are no verses or justification in the Quran for this belief, and they classify it as cultish. But for Omar, the claim that his religion, his form of Islam in its purest and most radical sense, would come back and rule the world became his substitute for the loss of identity and despair in search of a martyred cause.

Show me a true victim, one whose life was destroyed by consequences not at all of their own making, and I will show you the potential for a radical. The self demands dignity; dignity demands equality. This grants a cause, a cult or a tyrant the ability to convince the oppressed that the loss of their dignity comes from a scapegoat. To create a scapegoat, you must objectify them and dehumanize them. In my time with Omar, he identified many scapegoats. Americans, Western values, modern secularism, Sunnis, Jews and the liberal media. He felt oppressed, and he objectified certain groups to justify his terrible crimes.

However, persecution does not have to be as extreme as Hitler or Hussein. How we address individuals in our society, the respect we give to all dignities, the messages they hear through social media, the nightly news, the pressure from political correctness, changes in the workplace or even the stories we tell ourselves can lead to a feeling of invisibility. And trauma is individual. You can compare the effects of trauma, but you cannot compare one trauma to another and expect the one with less trauma to be grateful.

Before becoming a psychologist, my journey began in the deserts of the Middle East, where I would begin to understand my parents' journey. As Jews in Iraq, they could attest firsthand to real oppression, murder and genocide. From understanding their lives and their oppressors, I gained an ability to veil my inner feelings and connect to people like Omar. I also began to understand how decisions made thousands of years before could have an effect and might even become one's destiny. And so, my fate or my destiny began with my journey in the deserts of Egypt.

3

DANCING IN THE SANDS OF EGYPT
MAY 1999—CAIRO, EGYPT

O n the hot dusty streets of Cairo, the noon call to Islamic prayer (the adhan) was beginning. Loudspeakers had been installed on the tall minarets in modern times to ensure that everyone knew when the prayers were beginning. The prayer given by the muezzin is an art form. Historically, the muezzin recited the prayer five times a day from the minarets, the beautiful towers on the mosque, and it created the exotic feeling that one gets in Arabic communities where Islam is the prevailing religion. The streets emptied as Muslims focused on the prayer. As others disappeared, I walked under the ancient buildings, with laundry lines crossing the street providing some needed shade from the scorching sun.

While I am Jewish, I can easily be mistaken for Arab. My face is oval, with pronounced eyebrows and very long eyelashes over almond-shaped eyes. My complexion is dark, especially after sun exposure. I have long, curly, thick hair and full lips. I also have a long Arab-looking nose, but if one looks closely, you can see the hook at the end.

While studies have been done showing that hooked noses

are not necessarily affiliated with the Jewish population, it became a trait associated with Jews because of Nazi propaganda in the 1930s, and thus an "undesirable" feature. Nonetheless, I look Arab because I am Arab. I am an Arab Jew. My Jewish parents were born in Baghdad, Iraq. They were part of a very old Jewish community that would be terrorized, tortured, murdered and forced into exile while my parents were just teenagers.

On this day, I was looking for an important address. I was seeking one of the most famous belly dance teachers in the world, Raqqia Hassan, hoping to train at the feet of a master. Finding Raqqia in Cairo in 2000 was proving to be elusive. It would be almost a decade before one could pull out a cell phone and Google an address. And here in this ancient neighborhood of Cairo, not far from the shadows of the ancient pyramids, streets were often unnamed, and no building had an address. To find where you were going in this part of town, you had to ask people.

For a 20-year-old Jewish woman, I sometimes wonder why I was not more intimidated. I had learned the language in the months prior as I trekked across the Sinai Peninsula with little money. On my journey, I befriended a small shop owner who agreed to teach me the Egyptian dialect. From my parents, I had an Iraqi dialect, but it wasn't good enough to help me fit into the Egyptian community. By the time I got to Cairo, I may not have been fluent, but I had enough to blend in and intelligibly ask for directions.

Belly dancing was part of the culture I had grown up in. In my family, each generation of women handed down basic dance skills to their daughters and nieces. My mother had done the same. When Arabic music would play, the girls would display their newly acquired belly dancing moves while the others smiled and snapped their fingers, calling out encouragement. The dance was expressed to socially rejoice and celebrate at parties and gatherings, but I wanted more. I not only wanted to improve my dancing skills and master the art, but I was also looking for a deeper connection to who I was and where I came from.

Raqqia Hassan was a legend in belly dancing, and I had no appointment, no agreement for her to train me and little money to pay her. All I had was the desire to learn and the chutzpah to ask. But to do so, I had to find her and convince her that I was worthy of her time and training.

As I entered the building where Raqqia had her studio and her home, it looked exactly like one might imagine. The building was made of clay and soil. Wires were strapped to the outside of the walls, running down the hallways. The lights were just bare bulbs, most of which were blown out. The floors were too old to see if they had ever had any design on them.

The heat seemed to swell up inside the halls. Walking into her suite, the window air conditioner was loud, but the cool air was a relief. Raqqia was nothing like I thought she would be. She did not appear as glamorous as I anticipated, but of course, I was 20 years old and did not appreciate that she was more than a master of the art. She was a businesswoman. She wanted to know why I was there and what I wanted from her.

I told Raqqia I had very little money to pay for her private lessons and that I was just starting to train in my hometown of Vancouver with Rahma Haddad, a Lebanese artist. I told her that my family was from the Middle East and that I loved dancing and was determined to learn. I told her no one would work harder than me. I told her about my travels throughout Egypt and the rare and sacred encounters I had traveling throughout the Oasis towns and borderlands of Libya. She was not only impressed by my travels across the less journeyed sites of tourists, she was eager to learn all my impressions of these exotic places that she ashamedly admitted she had never experienced as an Egyptian. I am not sure how, but I won her favor, and she agreed to teach me at a very inexpensive cost if I would commit to the training.

For more than a month, the training was intense. She worked me like a professional athlete. Her real skill was creating choreography and then repeating moves again and again until I'd mastered them. She tied the movement in my hips, my torso, my abdominals, my legs, my arms and my hands to the beat of the music. My turns, smile and even my eyes followed the emotional tone of the rhythm.

She insisted that I understand the reason belly dancing existed. Not just the history but the purpose—and to her, there was both purpose and cause. She resented the dancers who demeaned the art and performed in cheap nightclub cabarets. She trained all the artists who were selected to perform on the prestigious Nile cruise ships with their own orchestra. She knew all the top musicians, who eagerly waited for her call to construct an orchestra for a night gala and showcase the best of the best talented and beautiful artists. She imbued power and protection over the art, but she was tough and demanding, which made her sought out by world-class dancers from Russia, Brazil and Europe. Everyone respected her and dancers tried hard to prove their worth to appear on her stage.

And there I was in her studio. She verbalized the perfect sounds of the dumbek, the Egyptian drum: *Dum, tak a tak, Dum Dum, tak a tak*. She would scorn me at my imperfect attempt to hit each rhythm with sharpness and clarity, staccato beats with fluidity and grace.

"You are doing it all wrong," she would say as she pointed and chuckled at my feet that pointed inward as I attempted to layer the movements while also strutting across her dance floor. "You are walking pigeon-toed!" She immediately corrected me. It was frustrating. I was expected to walk with my chest elevated, my arms outstretched and supple, my fingers extended yet delicately placed and an accentuated movements in my hips, all while strutting effortlessly across the floor with traveling steps. She explained the history and meaning of the various rhythms, including Taqsim, Baladi, Saidi, Ayub, Zar and Khalligi. Taqsim movements are slower and controlled and very sensual whereas Baladi and Saidi are of the country and more earthy, grounded and large. The Ayub and Zar have more tribalistic rhythms with gyrating movements and are used historically to exorcize evil spirits from the village. Khalligi represents Western African cultures with more hair tossing and whipping movements.

This was sacred knowledge and history. Belly dancing was influenced by other dance traditions all over the ancient world but also had been modified and enhanced for thousands of years. No one culture nor one era owns the art of belly dancing. It is as universal as a dance that exists on the planet. Belly dancing tells us something about ourselves that goes back to the earliest recorded moments of time.

Each rhythm change called for a learned artist to demonstrate to her audience appreciation through her technique to honor the call of the various rhythms and veiled meanings. It wasn't enough to simply be attractive or have the technique or even the knowledge. You had to embody the spirit of the art. I knew I lacked the former as a novice in training, but I had the spirit of the art inside of me, begging and beckoning me to reconnect with it. I knew it and she saw it.

After Raqqia Hassan's training, I journeyed into the sandy deserts of Egypt, where I had many more adventures. From practicing my new art around fires that lit the Egyptian sky to becoming a divemaster in the Red Sea, I felt I lived a lifetime in a very short period. It was there, dancing, diving and listening to the ancients where many of the lessons I would later use in psychology began to form.

But the first thing I did as I struck out on my own was purchase my first belly dancing outfit from a shop in Cairo's

Khan el-Khalili market. It was made of layered sheer deep blue chiffon and allowed the viewer to see the movements under-neath. Hundreds of stringed glass beads on the bra and belt reflected the light and shimmered as my body vibrated. I wasn't sure where, but I knew that somehow I was going to practice my art in the ancient Sinai desert.

Shortly after that, I got a job at a dive shop on the Red Sea, taking groups of foreigners to explore the wonders of aquatic life in one of the best dive sites in the world. And at the end of our dives, we sat around a campfire with Mt. Sinai in the back-ground and the Red Sea shimmering in front of us, and we discussed the many mysteries of this ancient land. At these fires, I began my first performances. They were not paid, but after our dives, around the fire, I practiced my art. During this time, I met Egyptians, Lebanese, Persians, Turks, Palestinians and Iraqis. I listened to their views of the world, of Islam, of Judaism, of women and of the US (usually with them never knowing I was Jewish or American). The dance itself became my veil.

Dancing in this area where Abraham once lived, where Moses ascended into the mountains to obtain the 10 Commandments, where my people, both Hebrew and Arabs, had occupied for millennia, my connection became spiritual.

As I would look up into the stars, I thought of my ancestors and the many hundreds, if not thousands, of Semitic people who had lived here in very different times and circumstances. Some suffered unthinkable tragedy and others were driven from their homes simply by nature of their identity. But all had reverence for this mountain, this sea, these skies and this dance that had the power to enchant them. I knew I had to tell their stories.

4

PRAYING FOR A MIRACLE
APRIL 1, 1974

لا تحرق قلبك بالحسد، ولا تقتله بالحقد، ولا تمرضه بالغل. عش سليم القلب مرتاح
البال، ودع الخلق للخالق.

Don't burn your heart with envy,
Don't kill it with hatred,
And don't make it sick with malice.
Live with a secure heart and contented mind.
Entrust the creation to the Creator.

-Arabic poem, author unknown

She had lost everything. She stood in the dusty ancient street of Baghdad, feeling terrified, angry and lost. The beautiful young Iraqi woman waited to see if the names of her family members were on the list of those who would be spared.

It was three years after the hanging of the nine Jewish men

(January 27, 1969), and many other Jews had been imprisoned, tormented, tortured or murdered. One of those Jews was my mother's father. It was my mother who waited in that town street for the list of Jews who could apply for passports and leave.

Many Jews had already fled the city while others were waiting it out in hopes to move their assets offshore. For this young woman and her brothers and sisters, this was no longer an option. All they had was taken by the state or the prowlers who fed upon the outcast. They were only hoping to leave with their lives. Months before, their father had been imprisoned. She wondered if by some miracle they would be granted passports so they could leave. She wondered if by some miracle her father might go with them. She cried as she thought about where her father might be and what pains he might be suffering.

∼

The Prison Qasr El-Nihaya (The Ending Palace)
Baghdad, Iraq—October 20, 1972, 18 months earlier

The sandstone walls created an echo through the prison. The dirt floor held the moisture and created a musty smell. The sound of dripping water could be heard beyond the moans and screams of men.

This was a place of evil.

The Ba'ath Party had come to power and was involved in a political genocide against the people they saw as enemies of the State. These men were chained to the wall and strung from the ceiling, and rotting bodies were strewn out on the floor. On the walls, men had inscribed their names into the sandstone. Ezoury could see one inscription that said, "Allah, please save me." He wondered if Allah had saved this man, or if his God, Adonai, would ultimately save him and his family.

Ezoury was my grandfather.

The captors had left hours ago, giving a reprieve from torture to the men in prison. There were no windows in the building, but you could hear the women outside screaming to see if their husbands, fathers or brothers were inside. The women could not know what was happening inside, but they knew that the Ba'ath Party and their tormentors could be incredibly inhumane and cruel. The women had seen it in the way they treated Jews on the sidewalks, the way men were hung in Liberty Square. They knew what was happening inside was worse than death for the people they loved.

The tormentors had hooked the prisoners' bodies to electrical currents. When the current rolled through their bodies, it forced their jaws to clamp down, their eyes to roll towards the back of their heads and their fingers and toes to violently curl into a tightened knot. Their muscles would involuntarily spam, exhausting every fiber of their bodies. When the tormentors stopped the current, the victims were not only left in severe pain but total exhaustion.

After the horrific shock that jolted every nerve in their bodies, the prisoners became terrorized by the anticipation of subsequent shocks. As the mind becomes weakened and overcome by terror, pain, shock and fear, the brain's limbic system, considered to be the reptilian part of the brain, overwhelms any rational thought or thread of character into pure survival mode, regressing into a shell of humanity. In these moments, people often express saying or doing things they never thought they would be capable of doing, shedding who they are to the most basic form of a human being. Electric shock is designed to reduce the human spirit to a primitive form through defeat, despair and dread, while other forms of torture are specifically designed to utilize the neocortex, the rational part of the brain. Most human beings' individuality is defined through the neocortex of the brain. However, the human spirit, not well defined, is used in our thinking to comprehend and appreciate more advanced forms of thought and a complexity that separates us from non-primates. These other types of torture are designed to utilize the neocortex by rationally making the prisoner comprehend that without the tradeoff of providing information, everything they love and care about will vanish.

The men torturing prisoners often have a variety of mental frameworks that enable them to harm another being in this gruesome way. A controversial study conducted by Philip Zimbardo in 1971 found that even moral people would engage in abuses of power. The famous Stanford prison experiment revealed that under particular circumstances and environmental pressures, an individual can deny the human rights of another individual,[1] but the abuse always begins with dehumanizing and vilifying them. While the scientific validity of Zimbardo's study remains criticized in psychological circles,[2] these elements of his study seem to be supported by Milgram's prior Agency Theory[3] and a 1961 study on obedience to authority.[4] There are a multitude of means and various levels of harm through dehumanizing a person that may include victimization. As we saw in the Iraqi prisons, their ability to take more severe measures in dehumanizing prisoners was available.

Torturing a man who is clean, well-groomed and presents like other people you know is much more difficult than torturing someone who smells, who is filthy, whose hair is disheveled or shaven, whose teeth are unclean, who begs or cries. These people are easier to torture because they seem less than human. As the tormenters entered the room, even with their sadistic nature, they were still appalled by the smell of feces, urine, blood, vomit and human filth.

The torturer may also be driven by a sense of cause. They believe that the cause is so great that it justifies what is happening to the men in front of them. And if that person is dehumanized, it's even easier. Their desire to torture may also come from a different mindset. People filled with pain, angst, envy and vengeance derive a purpose from torturing the person in front of them. For some, they can even derive sadistic pleasure.

Before someone can treat other humans this way, they not only have to dehumanize the victims, they have to begin to dehumanize themselves. The ability to dehumanize yourself begins with ideology. It can seem innocent at first, yet ideology starts with the simple process of taking the good and evil inside each of us and exporting the evil to an outside group. This relieves the individual of their accountability for treating the other person badly because the other person is evil. Once this mindset starts, it is addictive. It is through labels that we place on others that we begin to dehumanize who we are.

For an Iraqi torturer doing Hussein's bidding, it helped if the person they were abusing was a Jew, a threat or a traitor, but it was not essential. For these tormenters, the essential part was to gain a sense of power over another human being, to express a fierce rage or to derive a demented, remorseless sense of plea- sure through harming another human being.

For them, the challenge was in making certain that they didn't go too far early on in the interrogation, that they did not kill the prisoner before the necessary information had been gathered. The likelihood of false confessions increases with torture. The longer someone is tortured, the less of a sense of reality they have. All a prisoner has left is a primitive instinct to survive. The prisoner will do anything, say anything to stop the excruciating pain from going through their body. At some point, almost all people will break. And when they do, they will give up anything, regardless of who may be hurt by it. When that fails and the tormentor continues to torture them, they will then surrender information that may not be true. For Ezoury, the torturers were most interested in where he had hidden his money.

What is the psychology of torture? What is the purpose?

While the success ratio may be low, there are still people working in intelligence who use these methods to gather information. According to the 2014 intelligence report, US intelligence forces informed and led by two psychologists[5] believed that torture could be utilized to gather the information that could prevent another 9/11 attack.

Ironically enough, this torture inflicted upon suspected terrorists by American troops occurred in the very same prison system in Iraq where Jews were tortured decades before. In the late 1960s and early 1970s, as vice chairman of the Revolutionary Command Council and formally al-Bakr's second-in-command, Saddam Hussein took over internal security, which included running prisons where men like Ezoury were tortured. Prisons like Qasr El-Nihaya or Abu Ghraib were both infamous Ba'ath Party prisons used later by the US. It should be noted that significant studies were done to determine whether Abu Ghraib actually provided useful intelligence to the US. Senator John McCain, a former prisoner of war and survivor of torture, helped lead an effort to ban the use of torture and showed that very little actionable intelligence resulted from it.[6] Information gathered from torture has been proven to be unusable and not dependable intelligence. This begs the question of whether the real purpose is to satisfy the needs of those inflicting the torture.

Prisoners were tied with their hands handcuffed behind their backs, suspended from the ceiling from a chain. This prevented them from being able to rest or lay on the ground. As they became weaker and their bodies began to fall forward, the chain pulled from the shoulder sockets, sending excruciating pain throughout the whole body. Over time, with immense exhaustion, the rib cage stretched and the lungs filled with fluid, creating the feeling of drowning. The compulsion to cough brought on a pain that made the rib cage feel like it was about to burst. This kept prisoners awake and in terrible pain for hours at a time. This was the fate of Jewish men like Ezoury who would end up in these Ba'ath prisons. The prisons were one-way doors, or as the prison's name indicated, this was the ending palace, not designed to reform but to extract confessions from the prisoners and provide revenge or booty for the tormentor.

On the outside, Ezoury was a well-known jeweler. He had a large family of eight children, and he was the financial supporter for them, his in-laws and his own brothers and sisters. He had committed no crimes against the State other than being Jewish and wealthy. Ezoury never stood trial, which leads to the obvious conclusion that they had found no information that they could convict him on. The more obvious goal of the abductors was to rob Ezoury of whatever wealth he had. When Ezoury's family arrived at his jewelry shop, it was obvious that the abductors had ransacked his business. Allegedly, this is where Ezoury kept his cash. The family believed that there may have been other offshore money but whatever wealth may have existed disappeared with Ezoury. If Ezoury had the ability to still think rationally after the torture, he undoubtedly would have been willing to give up whatever he had to save his family.

In one of the rooms in the prison, the Ba'ath Party tormentors readied themselves to begin torturing a variety of prisoners. Saddam Hussein himself would regularly be amongst these men to join in what they called "torture parties." They tortured men in a variety of ways. Tying electrical wires to their eyelids or their scrotums. Tying a string on the end of their penis and forcing the captures to drink gallons of water, causing their bladders to burst.

Outside, an anonymous graveyard held the bodies of those killed by the Ba'ath Party. A group of former inmates, calling themselves the Free Iraqi Society, has assembled mass amounts of information on this organized atrocity. In most cases, the Ba'ath Party kept information on the people they tortured. For some, you could only find a name and a date. For others, there was a location on the gravesite. In Ezoury's case, all information was erased, leading one to believe that whatever happened to Ezoury's wealth was more self-serving to the captors than a matter of State policy.

~

BASRA, IRAQ
1898

My grandfather, Ezoury Menashi Moshe Shamash, was born in 1898. He was the third of eight children and the first-born son. Ezoury's parents were very poor. When Ezoury was 16, the entire world was at war, and Iraq was under Ottoman rule. The Ottomans, in World War I, sided with the Central Powers, unified as part of Austria-Hungary and Germany. This would result in the breakup of the Ottoman Empire when the Central Powers were defeated, but not until they had lost 325,000 young men.

Rome and the Byzantine Empire came to an end at the hands of the Ottomans. The Ottomans sacked Constantinople in 1453. The Conqueror, Mehmed II, seized the Christian capital and converted it to Islam, renaming it Istanbul. The

Ottoman Empire was one of the longest and most powerful dynasties, lasting more than 600 years.

The Ottomans converted large areas in the Middle East, Eastern Europe and northern Africa to Islam. The Sultan gained authority over religious and political structures. Non-Muslims were part of a millet system,[7] an independent court of law that gave minority groups the ability to still maintain their culture while under the Ottoman structure. Comparatively, Judaism prospered under Ottoman rule.[8]

At the beginning of World War I, the Ottomans began to put young men into involuntary servitude for the cause of the Ottoman Empire and the Central Powers. For Ezoury, the Ottomans enlisted young Jewish men and used them for what is known by officers as cannon fodder, men whose lives were so little valued by the government that it didn't matter if they were killed by their own cannons. They were sacrificial lambs for the Ottoman army. Spending his life in service to an Islamic empire seemed a waste to Ezoury and his family. Ezoury's parents knew that young Jewish men would be sent to the frontline and told him to run away instead of dying in war. Ezoury did exactly that.

When the war was over, the Ottoman Empire dissolved. After that, the Middle East was fragmented and the British and French colonial forces occupied the Middle East. This was by design to ensure the Arab rule could not again regain a unifying empire as it did with Ottomans, Persians and Babylonians in the Middle East. The Persians were located mainly in Iran, the descendants of the empire of Babylon were in Iraq and the oil was located mainly in areas that would become the Bedouin states of Saudi Arabia and Kuwait. This created a wave of political forces to ensure that the divide would continue and there would be no rise of an Islamic Caliphate.

Ezoury headed south on foot, from Baghdad to Basra. He walked more than 277 miles from one city to the next. Ezoury had nothing. He begged for food and water, slept in the fields and moved ahead in any way that he could.

Alone, homeless, and as a vagrant, Ezoury settled in the seaport of Basra, mingling among others there. Eager to build his own successes, Ezoury shamelessly approached established businessmen to learn from them. As fate would have it, there were Jews among these men in Basra. One of the men took pity on Ezoury and took him in as an apprentice to teach him a trade in jewelry repair. The shopkeeper bought, sold, fixed and traded all kinds of jewelry. Ezoury worked as this man's apprentice for years, learning the trade and becoming a talented craftsman. These entrepreneurial skills would assist him in developing his own successful merchant business years later.

When the war ended, Ezoury returned to his family in Baghdad. He had built a savings and used this to rent a small shop to open his own modestly-sized jewelry store. As the eldest son, Ezoury continued to provide his earnings to support his family. He created a dowry to help marry off his six sisters and felt burdened by this responsibility, yet was a proud man nonetheless. Ezoury was a self-made man—nothing easy was handed down to him and he worked hard for everything he earned. He was a just man who believed in fairness. He gave what he owed and expected the same in return. He was dependable and kept secrets private. People often confided in him and entrusted their life savings to him.

In 1945, at 47 years old, Ezoury had built a decent enterprise. He decided it was time to start his own family. He married an 18-year-old woman named Leoni Aziza Salman Yehouda. Leoni was a gorgeous Jewish woman, born in 1928. She also had an unspecified developmental disability, but her youth, beauty and shy demeanor were her defining characteristics. Her parents considered Ezoury, who was financially successful, a wonderful suitor who would be able to provide for her. After all of Leoni's siblings married off and left Iraq, her mother,

Ghergia "Nana" Kattan, moved into the Shamash household once her elderly husband died.

Just a few years before, the Farhud, also known as the violent dispossession, had erupted in 1941. In the 1940s, three percent of Iraq's population was Jewish, which amounted to almost 135,000 Jews. Jewish communities had existed in Iraq from the 6th century BCE, almost 1,000 years before Muslims. Under British rule, Jews enjoyed complete citizenship, but that began to change when the coup in Iraq favored the Central powers. By the time the British did come back to Basra on April 19th, 1941, the flames of antisemitism burned blue.

On June 1st, 1941 in Baghdad, British soldiers surrounded the city. Jewish citizens believed the threat from the pro-Nazi regime had passed. They began to venture out into the city to celebrate the traditional harvest festival of Shavuot. Angered Iraqi soldiers, police who had supported Rashid Ali al-Gailani's coup d'état and Fattuwa youths sympathetic to the central power instigated riots. Hitler had found a way to extend the Holocaust without firing a shot.

Dr. Jocelyn J. Bélanger from the Department of Psychology at New York University Abu Dhabi examined the addictive natures of ideological obsession. Bélanger concludes that ideological obsession creates destructive behaviors similar to addictions. The pursuit of political or religious ideology, like other addictions, consists of strong irresistible impulses, causing the afflicted to give up other activities in pursuit of one's ideology "despite it being both psychologically and physically hazardous." In addition, she called out how these ideological obsessions created a trend towards violence.

Ideological obsession creates four processes that drives one towards violence:[9]

1. It deactivates moral self-regulatory processes, allowing unethical behaviors to be carried out without self-recrimination.
2. Obsessed individuals are easily threatened by information counter to their ideology, which leads to anger and violent retaliation.
3. They are attracted to like-minded individuals who support ideological violence, leading to amplification of the violence.
4. They are susceptible to "psychological reactance, making them immune to communication strategies intended to dissuade them from using violence. In fact, messages espousing non-violence can have the opposite effect by reinforcing their violence-supporting ideology."

The atrocities of this period are incomprehensible. Witnesses talked about violent bands of men beheading Jews and bashing the skulls of babies. Edwin Black's *The Farhud: Roots of the Arab-Nazi Alliance in the Holocaust* documents the horrors. Murderers waived severed limbs and, in one case, the breast of a young Jewish woman. Perpetrators raped Jewish girls at local schools. During the riots, 150 to 180 Jews were murdered, 600 were injured and 1,500 stores were looted. An unknown number of Jewish women were raped.

Brain imaging studies of people addicted show decreased activity in the frontal cortex. This is part of how these atrocities make sense. But once this mindset is put in place, it is an addiction, and while one might suppress the addiction, they are not cured, only recovering. And eventually, a relapse is possible. Like alcohol and drugs, the best thing we can do is to recognize before we become addicted that ideology is not in our best interest. And in the case of the Farhud, it was just the first sign of a portion of a society addicted to a radical ideology.

The Farhud would last for two days. It stunned the Jewish citizens who were unarmed and unprepared to deal with the violence. Many tried to leave, but the Iraqi rules made it difficult. This would settle down, and under British rule, many Jews would go back to their lives and become prosperous. But it was a warning of what was to come—a warning that, in 1945, was not apparent to the young Ezoury.

5

IT WAS ALREADY TOO LATE

1952-1972—AL-MASBAH, A NEIGHBORHOOD
EAST OF THE TIGRIS RIVER

قمّة الصبر سكوت وفي القلب جروح متكلمة. وقمّة القوّة ابتسامة وفي العين ألف دموع منحدرة

"The pinnacle of patience is silence when in the heart many wounds are spoken, and the peak of that power is to smile when in the eyes there are many tears."

-Author unknown

The hangings in 1969 were not the first. While violence wasn't limited to harming the Jewish community, it was driven by an ideology bent on nationalism and racism. Often the target was other Arabs who refused to fully accept radical Pan-Arab views. The followers of such ideologies always believe the ends justify any means.

∾

Baghdad, Iraq
July 14th, 1958

Evelyn and her sister, Ferial, were startled by the loud noises outside their home. Ferial ran to the roof. They could hear what sounded like explosions, gunfire and the squealing of tires driving fast around the city. They spotted a truck driving around the area with a naked man's body tied behind it.

On July 14th, a group called The Free Officers, a secret military organization led by Colonels Abd al-Karim Qasim and Abdul Salam Arif, brutally deposed the Iraqi monarchy. After creating a secret organization inside the military, they initiated a coup that began with seizing the radio station, where they announced the revolution. Then they sent detachments to seize the Rihab Palace in Baghdad. King Faisal II, knowing he and his family were under assault, had his men stand down. It was a mistake that would cost him everything. He was taken to the courtyard and there, he, his wife, mother, the Crown Prince and other members of the Royal Family were told to face the wall. They were shot on the spot.

Qasim and Arif then set out to search for Nuri al-Said, the prime minister under the government. Al-Said was captured the next day on July 15th disguised as a woman. He was killed and dragged through the streets along with the Crown Prince, whose body was dug up, burned and run over so many times by buses that it was no longer recognizable. It was the dragging of al-Said behind a truck racing through the city that Evelyn and her sister heard on the streets that day.

The factors that led to the July 14th coup are by no means simple. The coup brought power to the rural mindset that produced tribal conflict, leading to internal oppression. These groups were certainly more affected by the recession and eventually, a depression gripped the country after World War II. In addition, the educational system had been radicalized with nationalist thinking that both Qasim and Arif were brought up in. Nationalism and Pan-Arab views were gripping much of the Middle East with the idea of one Arab world from Western Asia to North Africa, from the Atlantic Ocean to the Arabian Sea. And certainly, Israeli success in its conflicts with Egypt and Syria gave rise to an embarrassing defeat for Arabs against people they considered inferior.

The unintended consequences that come when the rule of law is overthrown are significant. Professor Shafeeq N. Ghabro at Kuwait University claimed that the 1958 revolution created the inability for political compromise. Leaders of the coup would eliminate those holding opposing views, create false charges against the enemy of the coup and confiscate property. It would cause significant human rights violations and eventually a mass exodus of hundreds of thousands of Iraqis who fled the country within four years of the 1958 revolution. It lead to the need for a real strongman, one who could suppress violent sects and crush opposition to the government—a tyrant who would rule with an iron fist.

By the time Evelyn was born in 1952, hangings and oppression of Jews were already a pattern in Iraq. The creation of Israel had made it worse for Jews in Arab countries. But what was not clear from the July 14th revolution was how the rise of nationalism could lead to genocide. From the fall of the Ottomans, Arabs were searching for new enlightenment and a renaissance of their culture. Ba'athism was born from Arab nationalism and Pan-Arabism. Israel was a threat to that state, and Jews were seen as the secret cabal that undermined an Arab society that was free and united. It threatened the identity of Arabs, causing them to ask, *Who am I?* And that would lead to an addictive ideology that would devastate Evelyn's and Joe's families.

The fascist Ba'athist movement, founded in Iraq and Syria, found a continual strawman in Jews. Politicians wanting to galvanize power would whip Arabs into a frenzy over Jews who they thought were spies or who they thought had stolen their dignity. As this movement was similar to Nazi Germany, Jews around the world, especially in the US, began to fund operations to save the Babylonian Jews who remained in Iraq. By the 1950s, Operation Ezra and Nehemiah[1] was in place and many Jews were leaving for Israel. It was estimated that approximately 150,000 Jews were left in those years.

Ezoury had visited Palestine in the 1940s. As far as he was concerned, there was nothing there, just desert and no opportunity for prosperity. Ezoury did not envision a plan to uproot and relocate his family at least until the 1970s. It was not the first time that Jews had been oppressed in Iraq, and he thought it would pass. He decided to remain and keep his family in Baghdad.

~

Baghdad, Iraq
1970s

Evelyn grew up in a home that was affluent. She lived among wealthy Arabs and had Muslim friends. Servants took care of dinner, laundry and cleaning, long after Operation Ezra and Nehemiah had run its course.

The home Ezoury raised his family in was a rental. Ezoury knew that owning real estate as a Jew was a big risk in Iraq, as the ownership could be seized at any time by the government. So the better position was to invest money in other assets and lease real estate. Ezoury's last home was in a great neighborhood, Al- Masbah, east of the Tigris River.

This residence had a bedroom downstairs, a shower room and a separate toilet room adjacent to a small hand wash sink. The family room had a TV and the only air cooling system, where the family would take naps on the floor in the hot Iraqi summers. The home had a nice living room that was only used when the family had guests. A spacious dining room boasted a very large dining table that comfortably seated 12 people.

Arabic families are big, with lots of people living in the same household. Ezoury had eight children, including five sons and three daughters, living in his home. In addition, his maternal grandmother and a live-in male housekeeper had their own quarters with bedrooms and toilets in a separate living area outside the main house. He had a gardener once a week, and a live-in nanny when there was a baby. A woman came once a week to wash clothes, and the big yard constantly had laundry hanging out to dry. The large, split-level home had a big, flat roof they could sleep on in the summer to feel the cool air from the Tigris River.

The house was full, but it was the marvel of many people in the Jewish community. Ezoury's children always had friends wanting to stay the night. And they had access to the best education, including the oldest son who, in 1964, went to Edinburgh, Scotland to receive his degree in medicine.

Once, a group of neighborhood Muslim children stood by the Shamash household fence, picking oranges from the tree that overhung the sidewalk, laughing and throwing the fruit in a disruptive manner. These children frequently came to the house to pick on the younger Shamash children because they were Jewish. Ezoury was wise and could see the innocence of children being corrupted by politics. One of those children was a young girl who often repeated antisemitic phrases taught to her by her mother. As an intervention, Ezoury confidently picked the fruit from his tree and, in a generous gesture, handed them to the children. It quieted down the girl and the others who were unsure of his motives. Ezoury hoped it showed that he was a just and likable man. But the young girl was simply an omen of what was to come.

On Thursdays, Ezoury went to the food market to shop for
the week. The Shorja center, or marketplace, was an almost
magical place where stores were concentrated in one area,
creating an excitement that only an Arab market can.

The narrow streets were paved, and small stores adorned
both sides of the road. People from everywhere walked down
the middle of the street. In the rare cases that a car drove by, the
driver would have to honk the entire way to get the walkers to
give him room to pass.

One could hear shop owners yelling from all sides and
talking to each other from across the streets. Others shouted,
trying to sell things from wagons in the middle of the road.
Mothers yelled at their children not to leave their side.

Off the main street there were branches of smaller streets,
which were also full of shops. These streets were crooked and
filled with potholes. People threw garbage everywhere, so one
had to be careful about where they were going and what they
were stepping on. Shop owners would throw water in the street
for good luck, to kill a little of the smell and to cool the area in
front of their storefronts. The streets were also covered with
tarps to protect the walkers from the summer heat.

One street was filled with stores of beads, while another
focused on shoes or books, and another on aluminum and
brass items. All day long, you could hear the hammers making
goods there and in the silver and gold market where you could
buy jewelry. The noise was so loud it could give you a headache
after a while.

One would never go there alone for fear of getting lost. All
these areas were connected and one could walk from one to
another, but getting turned around was almost intentional as the
shopkeepers did not want customers to leave. One could not get
to all of the stores in one outing, as there was too much to see.

If you decided to go shopping, you had to specify which

market you were going to. Al-Rasheed Street was the main street into the market. It was the most modern and organized street, where electronics and electric goods were sold, and it led to all other streets in the market. It had two lanes of traffic and was always congested with cars and buses.

Whenever there was a procession, Al-Rasheed Street was used. This was a street where Saddam Hussein attempted a failed coup d'etat in his twenties. When it failed, he was able to blend into the crowd and run away to Egypt in order not to be prosecuted. The street and its inhabitants were prepared to hide the man who would become a brutal dictator. Menahaim Daniel, the Jewish elementary school where Ezoury's children were educated, was at the beginning of this street, surrounded by high walls and metal gates. It was hard to know if that was to keep the kids in or the crowds out.

Ezoury did not own a car. When he shopped for the family, he used a taxi and filled the trunk and backseat with groceries. He would shop on Thursday, and by Saturday, all the fruits would be gone. With his large family, it seemed they just could not get enough. The younger children learned to try and get their share early, eat everything on their plate and not waste any food.

The Arab family unit is important. Grandparents lived with their children and helped raise the grandchildren. Families would go outside their houses in the evening, stand by their gates and converse with other neighbors every day. This was the social structure that Arabs lived by. Ezoury, who lived in this neighborhood of Muslims, knew better than to hang out by his gate.

As Jews, he and his family knew some of their Muslim neighbors did not like them. Some were envious of them, so Ezoury and his family would walk to friends' houses or just walk with no destination in the evenings. The hope was to meet friends on the road who were doing the same thing. It was a daily event to go outside and walk the streets.

While Evelyn was in middle school in the mid-1960s, the State removed phone privileges for Jews. Evelyn remembers her father being instructed by the government to deliver the only phone they had in their home to a government facility. The Jewish health club was also confiscated. Evelyn said that by this time, "We were pleading with our father to leave Baghdad." It seemed that everybody was leaving. There was no future in Baghdad. She recalls, "As Jews, we were not permitted to study, work—there was no income, no prospects, no future." The social milieu was disappearing. As all their friends were secretly leaving, Evelyn's family felt tied, and there was nothing more they could do. Everything they knew was disintegrating.

The factors exiling Jews from their ancestral home were clearly based on persecution, antisemitism, instability, restrictions, oppression, loss of security, the government seizing bank accounts, seizures of money and confiscation of assets.

Claire was Evelyn's sister. She had grown up like Evelyn, in a sheltered life. She was a normal teenage girl, interested in fashion, concerned with boys and potential suitors and enamored of celebrities. Football (Americans refer to it as soccer) was a major sport in Iraq. One of the teams from the Ivory Coast in Africa held an event in Baghdad. Claire planned to be downtown with two friends that day and was giddy over obtaining the autograph of one of the players. Claire was charmed by one of the athletes and provided him with her address on a piece of paper. Claire was so star-struck by his attractiveness, fame and athleticism, that she didn't realize the harm she invited to her household. She was just a typical innocent and naïve young teenager. On the way home, it became clear that she may have made a mistake. Several secret servicemen were following her and her two friends. At some point, the teenagers recognized that they were being followed. Panicked, they went back to their homes as quickly as they could.

When Evelyn arrived at the house later from the movies, she was confused to find a secret service member keeping guard on the front porch of her house. She was startled and paralyzed by what she further discovered. Ferial had hosted a luncheon with her girlfriends that day at the Shamash household and they all were sitting tense, fearful and frozen in place in the family room. Evelyn's mother was quietly weeping. Men were ransacking the home. Evelyn was terrified and knew that this was a very dangerous moment for the family.

Evelyn soon realized that the autograph Claire had obtained from the young football player had created a question about whether her motives were of an espionage nature. Jews were not permitted to converse with foreigners. The government believed that any communication they would have with foreigners could undermine the Ba'ath Party through internal measures or even worse, by letting the outside world know about the atrocities being committed in Baghdad. The men who were ransacking the home were looking for evidence that Ezoury and his family members were spies.

When the men found nothing, they took 14-year-old Claire into custody. They escorted her out of the home as her brothers and sisters were crying and screaming about the fate that might behold her. Ezoury, his eyes filled with tears, said to his family, "I lost my girl."

There is no more terrifying act for a parent than to feel that they have been unable to protect their children. To not use everything in his power, including physical force, had to be debilitating to Ezoury as his daughter was apprehended and removed from the home. But Ezoury had to know that any resistance would endanger the lives of all of his children. And so as the government began to oppress Jews, Ezoury's power as a father, and as a man, was being choked.

What ultimately saved Claire is still a mystery today. One theory is that a neighbor, who was a government official and had some powers in the regime, had been contacted by Ferial. Ferial frantically went to his house and personally requested that he help release Claire. Miraculously, within a few hours of Ferial's communication with her contact, Claire was released after being interrogated by the secret servicemen.

On a family outing in 1971, Evelyn was invited by her father to join her eldest sister Ferial and Ferial's new husband Kamal. They went up north for a few days to Mosul, Kirkuk and Erbil and ended up in a Kurdish town. At the time, Evelyn believed it was just a way to spend time together with the family. But in hindsight, Evelyn realized that Ezoury was planning an escape route and may have been scouting out a path with Ferial's husband. In fact, shortly after this trip, Ferial and her husband covertly escaped Baghdad through Turkey with valid passports, then sought asylum in Israel. Earlier that year, Evelyn's second eldest brother, Sabah, was smuggled out of Baghdad to Iran through Kurdish territory, the same passage Joseph was smuggled through in 1971 as well.

In the summer of 1972, Evelyn's maternal grandmother told Ezoury that she wanted to leave Baghdad and live with her son in London. After Claire's engagement party, Evelyn's grandmother went to London, accompanied by Evelyn's younger brother, Salman. They left Iraq for London shortly after Claire and David's wedding engagement. Salman's plan was to reunite with his brothers, Sabah and Kamal. The grandmother was the matriarch of the household and her departure foreshadowed the trauma and tragedy that would fall upon the Shamash family.

There was a silent mass exodus within the Baghdadi Jewish community.[2] Whatever the case may have been for Ezoury, he would have been pressured by being the sole provider for his family, his wife who had a developmental disability, as well as encumbered by his own fears, uncertainties and doubts about relocating en masse. Ezoury was cunning; he had a male secretary who spoke several languages and had previously placed his eldest son in school in Scotland. Yet despite his efforts, it became apparent that he had waited too long. At this time, Evelyn, her two younger brothers Menashi and Alber, her mother, her father and her recently married sister, Claire, were the only ones remaining in Baghdad.

Evelyn was approached by two suitors during the summer of Claire's engagement. One of them, she recalls, loved her dearly. But when her father asked for Evelyn's opinion about being wed to him, she declined because he was too old. The other suitor, she recalls, was a handsome man with deep eyes and long eyelashes who was liked by many women. He was appropriately nicknamed Prince. In accordance with tradition, Prince sent a trusted representative on his behalf to proposition Ezoury in the coffeehouse for Evelyn's hand in marriage. When Ezoury asked Evelyn for her opinion, she again declined, but this time on the basis that she believed his intentions were impure and not out of love, that he was after the generous dowry previously given for her two older sisters. Evelyn, born on October 21, 1952, was the fifth of eight children and had not yet turned 20.

While Claire found her true love match that summer, Evelyn soon discovered that hers had been there all along.

6

THEY TOOK HIM ON HIS DAUGHTER'S WEDDING DAY

OCTOBER 7, 1972

Despite all the losses, fears and instability, there was joy and excitement for Ezoury's family on the evening of October 7, 1972. Claire and David had been married on October 5th, and this evening marked the Motza'ei Shabbat (Saturday leaving) after the nuptials when, according to Jewish Iraqi customs, family and friends gathered at the couple's home to wish them well. The newlyweds lived with David's parents in their rental house. It was a celebratory time, yet looming with uncertainty—a moment of reprieve from the pain, silence and torment that filled the Jewish community at the time. Evelyn hoped nothing would go wrong.

She rushed to get ready and look her best. She was responsible for getting herself, her mother and her two younger brothers to the gathering on time. Ezoury was going to join them later; first, he planned to attend his regular backgammon game at a bustling coffeehouse on the Dijhla River. This weekly event was not just a place for the Jewish men of the community to congregate, drink Arabic tea and smoke nargilah. Communication of vital events, community news and business deals often transpired among Ezoury and his trusted friends in this space. Evelyn's younger brother, Menashi, pleaded to go with his father before leaving, but his father refused, saying he would meet them later at David's house.

As Evelyn showered upstairs, she opened the window to let the hot steam out, catching a glimpse of her father walking down the street and turning the corner. Though she had no way of knowing at the time, this would be Evelyn's last image and final living memory of her father. Moments later, an unmarked car carrying three men, members of the Ba'ath Party, would grab Ezoury and push him into the vehicle. These details were later informed by a local shopkeeper who had witnessed the abduction. The facts and evidence following Ezoury's disappearance remain a mystery but it is known that he was imprisoned, tortured and never seen or heard from again. In fact, his identity appears to have been wiped clean by the local government in suspected efforts to conceal the crimes committed against humanity.

Unaware of her father's fate, Evelyn put on her best dress and took a taxi with her family members to Claire and David's home. When she arrived, everyone asked her where her father was. The fact that Ezoury was not there was a bit scandalous, and some of the guests started asking if Ezoury was not pleased that Claire had married David. After several hours, Evelyn went back to her home to see if her dad was there. He wasn't, and she began to worry.

She hurried back to David's house and told the family that Ezoury was not home. David called a taxi and they started going from one house to another, asking friends if anyone knew Ezoury's whereabouts. They went to the main hospital and even the morgue. They could not find him anywhere.

At midnight, they went to the home of one of Ezoury's good friends. They sat and talked until the early morning about what their options might be and about who might know where Ezoury was.

For two days, they asked everyone about Ezoury's where-abouts. Finally, on the second day, David and Evelyn went to Ezoury's office. Ezoury had a safe where he kept his cash, the family jewelry and important documents. They knew the family needed the money to survive.

But as David and Evelyn walked through the busy market towards the office, they found the front office door was taped by police. David knew immediately what was happening and told Evelyn to quickly walk away. If they went into the office, what-ever fate had befallen Ezoury would ensnare his children. They walked quickly and silently through all the narrow streets, staying close to one another. When they reached the main street, David told Evelyn to go straight home.

Whatever was in that safe was already taken by the police who searched the building, including the life savings of a teacher who had trusted Ezoury. That teacher lost everything and later took his own life.

Evelyn and Claire continued looking for their father. On the other side of the Tigris River was an infamous prison known as Qasr al-Nihaya (The Ending Palace), which held political pris-oners. It was named this because those who went in never came out, and it was located near Saddam Hussein's palace.

Evelyn decided to take the bus alone to the internal security headquarters, knowing that she ran the risk of being arrested. As a woman and a Jew, walking in that street was extremely dangerous. She was met with disapproval by two men in a car who focused their stern gaze upon her. She avoided eye contact with the men and continued to the secret service headquarters.

At the headquarters, there were many women waiting to talk to someone about a family member who had disappeared or was in jail. All of them were wearing an abaya (a loose-fitting full-length robe worn by Muslim women). Most of the women were crying and pleading to see someone. Evelyn was the only one dressed in casual clothes. A man in a dishdasha (a light

long-sleeved collarless garment worn by Muslim men in the
Arabian peninsula) approached her and demanded to know
what her business was there. She told him she was looking for
her father who had disappeared. Astonished at her audacity, he
ordered her to leave right away and immediately return home.
From the look on his face and the tone in his voice, she understood that this was both a threat and a warning.

After the other siblings departed Iraq and the remaining
sisters were married and out of the house, Evelyn was now the
eldest in charge of the welfare and survival of the family. She
had her two younger brothers, ages 12 and 10, and her mother
who had a developmental disability. The rest of her siblings
and family members had departed by passport or been smuggled through borders via Tehran. At night, Evelyn could hear
her mom weeping softly so as not to disturb the children.

Since that Saturday when her father disappeared, all of
the remaining family members in the household slept
together in one bedroom. They were terrified, in shock and
disbelief at losing their patriarch, their rock, the one who had
held it all together and provided comfort, reassurance and
stability. Now all they had was one another. With Ezoury
gone, they had no money or means to procure an escape plan.
David stepped into the vacuum that was left by Ezoury's
abduction and tried to help as best as he could. He provided
what money he could gather to make sure the family was
eating. As the family became more desperate, they began to
quietly sell the goods in the home. Evelyn sold all the fine
handmade Persian carpets, including the one she had loved
sleeping on as a girl.

It was important to keep the financial situation quiet. Once
people began to recognize they no longer had money, they
would not receive assistance. They would have to depart the
family home in secrecy with few personal belongings. Yet, they
needed help from people to obtain a passport to leave the

country. From time to time, Evelyn attended her college classes so the students would not suspect what was going on.

David became a godsend for the family. He was important not only for what he physically provided but for the direction and support he gave them that was so necessary to survive. David told them that they should leave the house when the owner came and asked for the rent. He found another small rental home and provided the money for Evelyn, her younger brothers and her mom to rent it.

David and his family knew that what happened to Ezoury was writing on the wall for the remaining Jews in Baghdad. David's family all had passports and already escaped. He and Claire also had passports, but David decided that he could not leave Evelyn and her remaining family alone.

It is impossible to know what really happened to Ezoury, not even who the men were who forced him into the car. This not-knowing is a pain felt to this very day by Evelyn and her family. They will never know if he was even alive at the time they escaped Baghdad, or if there was more they could have done to save him. Every sibling individually blamed themselves for Ezoury's disappearance and agonized over what they could have done differently to change the fate of their father. Of course, as with any crime, the person to ultimately blame is the one who is responsible for the crimes themselves. There was no way to barter with the evil that would eventually take Ezoury's life. And there was no power or control any of the children could have exercised to prevent Ezoury's abduction, torture and imprisonment. One thing is for certain: the Jews who were abducted by the Ba'ath Party met painful ends. Ezoury undoubtedly suffered for the sole reason of being a Jew.

∼

The story of Ezoury being tortured is the most painful part for my family to relive. Yet, it is an important part of our family history and Jewish history, and I do not want to foster injustice by glossing over the details of my grandfather's last living moments. The reason for this is that these inhumane atrocities can very easily occur again—in the most unsuspecting times and the most unlikely countries.

While the descriptions of the prison and the torture methods come from credible sources, historical records and declassified CIA reports,[1] what specifically happened to Ezoury after his abduction came from the collected nightmares of his children and grandchildren.

Leaving Ezoury behind was a pain and torture to the family that transcended generations. They never knew if they had left him alive or dead. Evelyn dreamed of her father coming to her, trying to pacify her greatest fear, that she had left him there alive. Ezoury told her that he was tortured by three men who beat him while he was suspended from the ceiling.

My grandfather appeared to me in many dreams throughout my life despite my never having met him. I cannot be certain if these visitations came from the scars of my mother losing her father or if he really had reached out from the after-life to let me know what had happened to him. In my dreams, Ezoury sits on a small stool, stripped of his clothing, his pride, his dignity and everything he had built with his own hands. The room is underground, cold, wet, dark and bare. He knew that as long as he stayed alive, his family remained in harm's way.

～

The Ba'ath Party and Saddam Hussein controlled the national government. The official policy of the party in the 1970s was to encourage Jews to leave without their property, their possessions or their money. To encourage them to do so, the Ba'ath Party used very public displays of intimidation, threat, torture and hangings.

As mentioned in a previous chapter, Hussein himself, as a political leader, was known to take part in "torture parties" in Baghdad in the 1970s.[2] However, no holocaust or genocide happens with one man.

Historically, genocides happen as part of a mass movement. It may not even be noticeable at first. But the key is a political constituency that is completely conformist, thus making the public complicit.

Once the demagogue convinces the public that the pain they feel is caused by the immigrant or the invader, he can then begin to dehumanize them—shave their hair, strip them of their possessions and castigate them in public. And once they are dehumanized, some portion of the public will gladly join in to strip the "alien" of all that matters.

The Ba'ath Party policy was to force Jews to leave and to sequester their wealth for the state. The party saw this as a way to gain revenue for the movement and hold onto political power. However, at a local level, many officials had little interest in enriching the state or the party. Their goals were more self-serving.

Ezoury was affluent. That was clear from his reputation and the neighborhood he lived in. If the men who picked up Ezoury were local law enforcement, secret servicemen or officials of the local government, they did not need a warrant or even a judge's permission to pick him up as a potential enemy of the state. They had that ability on their own.

In tyrannical governments, authority to abuse human beings does not need to be ordered by the state. If enough political pressure exists, the state may stop the local officials from prosecution or incarceration. But without that pressure, it is easy to discriminate at will against someone, given even a small amount of power.

It is a good guess that the men David and Evelyn saw at Ezoury's office had gotten Ezoury to tell them where his financial resources were, and his wealth was more than likely divided up among them. It was most likely not redistributed to the state. Once they had the money, it was important that no trial take place. A trial could result in the state knowing these men had stolen the money for themselves. If this was true, then the best bet for these men was to get rid of the remaining family members or to have a passport magically appear for them. With his family gone, it could be as if Ezoury had never existed, which would have been the goal of his capture. The men involved in Ezoury's disappearance went far beyond the actions of an organized state. It spoke to the injustice that can exist in the hearts of men.

Ezoury spent a lifetime learning a trade and using it to build a decent life. It was an injustice that all the financial resources that Ezoury had spent his life earning ended up in the hands of men whose only skill was to torture. It was an injustice that Ezoury was not provided a dignified Jewish burial, and that his family would never know his fate. It was cruel that they would pick the day of his daughter's wedding celebration to abduct him.

My ancestral Jewish lineage had existed in Baghdad from the days of Daniel thousands of years earlier. They were integrated into the history. The biggest injustice was that these families could be eliminated as if they had never existed. Their names were wiped from the official records. But for Ezoury, he would have been relieved just to know his family had made it to safety. It is an injustice that he died afraid for their lives.

～

I still find it difficult speaking to my mother and father about what they would see as a genocide of Jews in Iraq. Ezoury was a humble and dignified man. He valued family, connection and stability.

His virtues were patience, confidence and persistence. And yet, he lived at a point in history and a place and time where the only option seemed to be to abandon all that he owned and all that was familiar to him when he saw warning signs all around.

Nonetheless, this is Ezoury's story. It is the story of a man who conquered a great many obstacles in his life to evolve into a success. He raised a large family in a place where, for thousands of years, his people, the Jewish people, had been a prominent part of the community. And those lessons that life gave him, that forced him to hang on and be persistent in hopes that the world would get better, all worked towards his demise.

There is one great lesson from this that I have never been able to overlook: how a society can dehumanize a group of people, and through that process, begin to commit unimaginable atrocities. This is only possible when one person begins to objectify another. The ability to establish in one's mind a label or a term that helps to objectify another leads to the internal justification of abuse.

The instinct to objectify those with whom we disagree is potentially one of the most damaging things that we can do to ourselves and that of a societal order.

When we objectify people, we are effectively betraying ourselves. After we have treated someone in a way that we know we should not, we apply labels to them, which becomes our justification for the harm that we cause.

It was clear in Iraq in the 1970s that the Ba'ath Party had created a justification for being antisemitic. They villainized Jews by calling them spies and traitors who would destroy their

way of life. They saw Jews as immigrants, enemies and disconnected from Arab culture.

When that objectification became complete, Jews became
less than people in the mind of the average Arab. Only the
stories told by the survivors can do justification to illuminate
the atrocity that unfolded.

Evelyn had one more year of college left to graduate, but that
was the least of her concerns after her father was abducted.
While Evelyn attended college so the students would not
suspect anything, her real goal was to get herself and her
remaining family members out of Baghdad. It was important to
conceal that her father had disappeared and that they were
planning an escape, as that might raise suspicion by the
government and be a reason for imprisoning other family
members. They were forced to live a lie for family preservation
in hopes of getting out alive. For five months, she went weekly
to check if the names of her family members were issued passports, allowing them to leave through secure and controlled
passageways. Eventually, the names of her remaining family
members were listed on the walls of a local government office
and issued passports. It was an exciting yet somber moment.

Before they left, David took one more shot at trying to see if
there was any chance Ezoury might be alive. He went to the
head of the Jewish community and they investigated Ezoury's
whereabouts to the best of their ability. David never told the
family what he learned. But he did tell them there was no hope
for Ezoury, and they had to leave.

The family felt pressured to go, but events kept happening
that seemed like Iraq would not permit them to escape. The
same week the family was issued their passports and bought
tickets to Istanbul, the youngest son, Alber, came down with

measles, a visible and highly contagious virus. The family knew they would not let him fly, so they disguised him as a young teenager with acne. Evelyn dressed Alber in reading glasses and clothing to make him appear older. Upon inquiry, Evelyn informed the male flight attendant on the plane that he had an allergic reaction to something he ate and they were permitted to board the flight that would be their passage out of Iraq.

On April 6, 1973, the last of Ezoury's family left Iraq, marking another significant historical exodus. Alone, stripped of the wealth Ezoury had worked so hard to provide, and even more tragically, without Ezoury, the family left the place that had been home for them and their ancestors for maybe 3,000 years.

When the plane landed in Istanbul, an Israeli spokeswoman greeted the family. She transported them by taxi to a hotel. Evelyn stayed in the room with Alber and nursed him back to health. When his condition improved, they flew to Tel Aviv on April 13, 1973.

As the family walked from the tarmac to the airport, they were greeted by David's brother. Evelyn, who had become the primary support for the remaining dependents, found herself pale, weak and in pain. She began to faint. The suitcase fell from her hand as she crumpled to the floor. David's brother lifted her back to her feet, took her suitcase and kept moving forward toward the immigration line. She was unsure if it had all finally hit her, the reality of the torment and trauma, or if she just found herself at that moment relieved of the tremendous stress she had shouldered for her family to get them all to safety. Whatever it was, or maybe even the combination of it all, was too much to bear mentally and physically.

An immigration resettlement agency put the family in a hotel for new refugee arrivals. Their lives started to shape anew. They had to learn the spoken Hebrew language, and Alber and Menashi were placed in school. While the stress of their lives being in danger was now behind them, Evelyn had no time to grieve or mourn the losses, but had to forge ahead and survive. She delved deep into a caregiver, provider and self-sacrificial role on that fateful Saturday, a role that she would continue to maintain for life, leaving behind a world she would never get back, marking the loss of her youthful innocence. She was struggling to live in a new country with a new language, a new culture and two younger brothers and a mother to take care of.

The Yom Kippur War erupted shortly after their resettlement, and the family went back to feeling their safety, security and mortality was yet again threatened as they had to endure the repercussions of violence, intergroup conflict and religious persecution. Every residence was equipped with a bomb shelter as the establishment of the State of Israel was forged on conflict. Evelyn panicked at the loud shrieking sounds of the sirens warning all civilians to take cover in their bomb shelters. And every time, she relived the panic and horror of the trauma she thought she left behind.

Evelyn's mom continued to silently weep almost every night, tormented by the past, devastated by her current reality and terrified of what was to come. Evelyn obtained a job to put food on the table and as days passed, they purchased a home opposite from Claire and David.

As Menashi and Alber grew older, Evelyn was ready for a family of her own. She became reacquainted with a young man named Joseph Bashah, a Baghdadi Jew who earned Evelyn's trust and heart.

Israel would become a place of rebirth.

7

MY JOURNEY TO PSYCHOLOGY
1999—THE WHITE DESERTS OF FARAFRA

I n a dusty, sandy camp west of the Nile River, in the middle of the White Desert of Farafra, we sat around the bonfire. The fire was only necessary for light, as the hot Egyptian air had us all perspiring. Our conversation was about changing the world and understanding one another.

I left home at the age of 19 to study art at the Emily Carr Art Institute in Vancouver, British Columbia, only to drop out after my first year. Much to the stress of my parents, I donated all my belongings and bought a one-way ticket to the Middle East, determined to see where I had come from and to answer the question, "Who am I?" I backpacked solo throughout Israel, Sinai, Egypt and Jordan. My parents did not pay for these trips. I saved up money by waitressing, and when my savings depleted later on my travels, I worked as a divemaster in the Red Sea in Dahab, Sinai.

I continued to belly dance there and, to the delight of the audience, I incorporated elements of fire dancing in my performances. While I actually improved in the art of fire dancing, I abandoned it after suffering some burns on my body that left scars. Dancing in the desert, by the fire and under the Milky

Way galaxy, I found a way to express myself through art, connecting to my ancestors and funding my continued travels and studies.

I lived among Bedouins in this Egyptian desert. We were on our way from Kharga and on a route that Herodias, "the father of history," called a "road traversed in 40 days." We were led by a family who was part of the Azazame Bedouin tribe that exists in the border towns between Israel and Egypt. These people are very dark-skinned, known for honesty and are very hospitable. The scarcity of grazing makes them nomadic. Right or wrong, they have been stereotyped as abductors of women.

The Bedouin we paid to navigate us through this desert left us with his eldest son to lead the group, a young Muslim man. Sitting around the fire, he wanted to know everything about America. He asked me many questions about the United States —how men and women acted, what we wore and the things we talked about.

On this night, however, we were all exhausted. All day, our Jeep continued to get stuck in dry quicksand. This would force all of us to get out and, for what seemed like hours, try to push the Jeep out of the sand. As a woman, I was required to wear a full head scarf and a black dress that covered my entire body. After pushing the Jeep, running to catch up to it and repeating this process every few miles over the blazing sand, we were completely worn out. At least, I was.

I lay on a hand-woven rug that night, watching the fire burn down to the red cinders. The sky was clear, with no ambient light from the ground. I could not only see the stars but the milky rings of our galaxy as well. I felt myself dozing off to sleep, listening to the crackling of the wood on the fire. As exhausted as I was, I was still amazed that I was here in this remote area of the Egyptian desert. With very little money, I was putting together a memorable journey and a lifetime of stories.

A short time after I dozed off, I felt a hand that started at the bottom of my black dress, sliding up my inner thigh. I was still asleep, but as the hand crawled up my legs, I opened my eyes and saw the young guide above me.

I started to scream. I scratched him, hit him, yelled and made as much noise as I could. The young guide was startled and ran away. I was shaken, confused about what to do and infuriated, but the exhaustion overcame me. All I could do in that moment was lay back down, cover my body with a thin veil and fall back asleep.

In the morning, I woke up with a renewed and vital rage. All the sexual harassment and objectification I had endured as a woman in the Arab world compounded upon itself and all I could think of was that I wanted to dismember our guide. I could not even think of the repercussions of injuring the only person who was able to get us out of the uninhabited desert or how the group would turn against me. I wanted to poke out his eye, pull out his hair and remove any chances of him experiencing sexual gratification again. I was going to war.

I screamed at the young guide and smacked him in the face. I shouted at him, calling him names—how dare he violate me and think he could get away with it. I told him that he would suffer and pay the price for what he did. I yelled that what he did was wrong and he should never again think he could do that to another woman. To my surprise, he smacked me back across my face, which only provoked me further. I lunged towards him, scratching his face. The other group members had to rip my claws from further injuring him. I am sure I looked like a wild animal, and in that moment, I was. The others in the camp hurried over and restrained us both, pulling us farther apart. While they were concerned about how upset I was, they were rightfully more concerned about me injuring our only way out of the vast and unmarked desert. There were no roads, maps or signs to follow. We were dependent on our guide, and he knew that.

What became more confusing and hurtful was that after I explained what the guide had done, the group turned against me, victim-shaming and blaming me. They accused me of flirting with him. By this, they were referring to me talking to him, asking questions about his life experiences and sharing mine. They accused me of not being culturally sensitive to the gender roles and expectations and that I was ultimately responsible for his sexual assault of me. The notion that he had no ability to control his sexual impulses was my responsibility, not his.

I was not going to let it go. I learned that lecturing our guide on women's rights, justice and gender equality would fall on deaf ears. Instead, I found the sweet spot that would emotionally torment and shame my guide. During the drive, in front of the others, I told him I was going to tell his father. This had provoked the emotional response I was looking for. He became terrified, panicked, weakened and remorseful. I found the consequence that would matter most for him: family dishonor and shame. I soon realized this was the most powerful tool for behavioral change that would hopefully prevent him from assaulting another woman.

He begged me not to tell his father. While in this state of mind, he even got into an accident, damaging the body of the Jeep. It was still operational, but now he was in a frenzy. The group was turning against him and upset about his service. By the time we returned to his town, he was in shambles. He begged me not to tell, and he cried like a small child, fearful of his father's punishment.

As the father of the guide appeared and saw the damage from the accident his son had incurred, his father slapped him firmly across his face, shouting and cursing at him in front of our group and the village. We all cringed at his father's outrage and physical abuse. I realized that his punishment would turn worse for him behind closed doors. The guide cowered to his father like an abused animal following every command and order from its owner. I did not have the heart to tell his father what happened. I took pity on him and just let it go.

What I came to realize was that, after all that had transpired, I felt confident that the young man would not assault another woman and believe he could get away with it. Between my reaction, the group's disapproval of him after the accident, his father's physical abuse, public shaming and family dishonor, I believe that even though the events of that day were not all related to the assault, they became intertwined in his mind. They certainly were in mine. I felt a sense that justice had been served. But I also wanted to uncover and understand this phenomenon further.

In the wake of the Me Too movement, so many women bravely shared their private and personal accounts of being sexually violated, exploited, abused and harmed. I felt the need to explore this more deeply in order to understand that what is the right resolution for some may not be acceptable for others. I know that I felt disappointed that the group did not support me and turned against me for their best interests. In my work as a psychologist, I know this is why many victims choose not to speak up or out against perpetrators. But this pattern is changing, with more protections afforded for survivors of assault, abuse and sexual harassment. None of these protections matter, however, if the abusers feel they are immune to consequences, if there is an unspoken and acceptable culture shielding the perpetrator and blaming the victim.

For the sake of preserving fairness, equality and restorative justice, the caution is that the pendulum swing should not overcompensate by swinging fully to the other side. There needs to be a balance, a middle path. I believe the solution is with changing cultural norms on sexual harassment, assault and abuse. For instance, if the situational safety permits, the ability for a person to raise their voice in the moment, draw attention from others, expose the abuser and the harm committed, and for the group of witnesses to join together in expressing disapproval for the harmful behavior, the greater the impact on changing social norms. The abusers learn that their behaviors will not go unpunished or shielded. These natural environmental consequences are powerful and restore the expectations and behavioral norms that society should be striving toward.

Over time, I have wondered if the young Islamic guide, who had no sexual experience, believed that what he was trying to do to me was something I would support. Or was his view that as a person, I didn't matter, and it was okay to assault me? Either way, he was not accustomed to even having discussions with women like the ones he had with me around the fire, much less to seeing women as individuals. The group discussion at the fire and my conversation with him directly might have been the closest he had ever been to being with a woman who spoke directly. He might have seen this as a form of flirtation and foreplay. In his worldview, Western women were liberated sexually. To him, he might have viewed me as encouraging his advancement. On the other hand, he may have viewed my values as so corrupt that as an individual, I did not matter, and he could do what he wanted.

In the West, we look to our criminal justice system for rule of law and social order. It is supposed to be fair to both sides to try and find the truth. While there is political pressure to make the system more geared towards the victim, I am not sure that tipping the scales of justice is good for society at large. I have evaluated both victims and victimizers, and rarely does a legal determination provide healing in itself. The impacts of the existing legal system on the lives of both the accused and the accuser are that it is almost impossible for either to admit fault or take responsibility. On this issue, the system is not serving our society or the individuals well. Our ideal should be to establish healing, balance of power and promote transforma-tion—the opportunity for the accused, if they are guilty, to offer an authentic apology and acknowledge the harm that has been committed. From a psychological standpoint, this can be more powerful than one who does not admit guilt but is found guilty. We can admit to ourselves that the standards between men and women are changing in America, but part of our goal should be to facilitate the change in a way that does not leave behind a wake of hate. The system should help promote the changing standard but also provide an opportunity for reflec-tion, change, growth, insight, behavioral modification and transformation.

Our ideal for restorative justice versus retributive justice has to rise above our emotions. We will not find the ideal other than in our minds and our thoughts. But we should search for the ideal. Platonic idealism points out that the ideal that exists in our mind is more true than the shadows we see here on Earth. Justice has to play many roles. One role is retributive: a punishment to the individual as well as removing the threat from society. The other role could be of a more restorative nature: to restore dignity, civility and courage, and to fulfill the promise each life has to offer. This should especially be consid-ered as it relates to minors, where restoration could offer a means to shape, inform, teach, model and correct the offensive behavior.

There is no silver lining to sexual assault. But this incident piqued my interest to understand different cultures, customs and behaviors of people. I did not lead with becoming a psychologist right away, but when I look back, I still find this experience to be formative in my thinking. I have strived to understand how different cultures affect our psychology. It helped form my interest in how we create extremists, victims, the radical right or the radical left, jihadists or terrorists. It increased my interest in people who are oppressed, and how the winds of political movements create outcomes not always to our liking. The event forced me to think about the paradigm of this man, and it forced me to think about mine.

Years later, that event in the sands of Egypt helped me better understand Omar. I was careful about my approach, my behaviors and my conversation. I had to not only honor Omar's culture but also to understand his limitations, his bias and his prejudices. The assault by the young Islamic man provided me insight into how others think, perceive and interpret information. I gained a better understanding of the process of dehumanization of others unlike us, of objectifying them so we can justify our actions against them. I was raised in a home environment where I was blessed. My parents were supportive, loving and encouraging. They provided me many opportunities for education, freedom and expression. They allowed me to make my own choices, although sometimes begrudgingly. I had only known the strife of life from listening to their stories, but as I took off on my journey across the world for many years, I discovered my own stories and my own struggles.

For someone to find meaning, they cannot remain in a victim mindset. They must believe that in at least some ways, they have the choice for self-determination and choosing their own destiny. Many of the people to whom I have provided psychotherapy have suffered horrific and incomprehensible traumas. Omar's condition is a product of a radicalization that came from the oppression of Saddam Hussein. The Shias, who knew they held the majority numbers in Iraq, were shamed by the Sunni Ba'ath Party controlling their government. This would lead to a nationalistic fervor amongst those who were oppressed. An Islamic radicalization simply would be inevitable for some percentage of this population.

When Hussein was finally captured, my mother described

that for her, it felt that justice had finally been served. Learning how he lived in a hole, eating out of a can, seeing him unshaven, unclean, weak, aged and vulnerable left the victims feeling somehow better. Yet after he was hung, the victims still felt the anger that came from their Arab friends and society turning on them. For them, they could not find peace from all the terror and trauma that had been committed, and retributive justice only offered a temporary solution, as it does not undo the harm that had been committed. I doubt the survivors will ever truly feel that justice has been carried out. For criminals like Hussein, there is no other place where his crimes could be better served than through an exposed trial and a sentence.

The response by most governments is to make the costs of taking part in these fundamental organizations high. They do this by imprisoning not only the violent offenders, but the leadership. And while there is some logic to this approach, it must be accompanied by some type of deprogramming and alternative ideology to have a chance at success. Replacing the radical Islamic view with an acceptable peaceful Islamic view is almost certainly essential in any deradicalization process.

Alas, for Omar, this would no longer be a considered option. For his crimes, prison was all that he could hope for. No one was going to change Omar's radical point of view nor even attempt to. But I saw a huge benefit in trying to understand the underlying causes which led him to a life of terror.

8

MY FATHER, JOSEPH BASHAH
JANUARY 27, 1969—BAGHDAD, IRAQ

لا يتم تسعير السعادة

Happiness is not priced.

-Arabic proverb, author unknown

My father, Joseph Bashah, was just 19 when he witnessed the hangings in Tahrir Square. He saw the wooden gallows that towered above the crowd. He could see the dead men hanging, their heads twisted to the side in grotesque angles. He heard the approval of the crowds. And while Joseph could not identify him, he could see the young Jewish boy who was his same age about to meet his death.

Joseph knew well that Jewish families like his were under assault. By 1969, the amount of Jews left in Baghdad was small enough that everyone basically knew everyone. He also intuitively understood that this crowd could easily turn on him or his family.

As fast as he could, he turned his bike around and left. He took the road by the Tigris River. It was longer, but far enough away from the park that he would be safe from the crowd. When Joseph got home, the television was covering the hangings. It was January 27th, 1969. The time for Jews to leave Iraq had long passed.

Young Joseph and his family had been home in Baghdad all their lives. By the 1950s, Jews were being exiled en masse to save their lives. By 1969, it was beyond unsafe for Jewish families to be there, despite he city being home to their families for over 3,000 years.

The Cradle of Civilization

This area where young Joseph rode his bike was along the same river that had deposited silt on top of soil for millions of years, giving rise to the first known civilization along the Mediterranean. A wealth of crops could be grown here, earning it the name the Fertile Crescent, while the rivers provided transport avenues for goods. Great empires would spring forth and fight to control this area, spending significant resources to conquer.

The name Mesopotamia means "the land between two rivers." It would spawn ancient societies in southern Iraq from 5,000 BCE and last until the 6th century BCE. It was here that, over 3,000 years ago, the Sumerians created the first known system for writing and thus recorded history. Using triangular-tipped instruments, they would make wedge-shaped impressions in soft clay. Eventually, this would evolve into some of the great religious literature and even the Code of Hammurabi,[1] one of the greatest early examples of judicial writings.

From this Cradle of Civilization sprang the Babylonian Empire in 1800 BCE. It became a prize for the Persians,

Alexander the Great, the Romans and then the Persians again. It eventually became subsumed by the Islamic Empire.

The Jewish History of Babylon was almost as long. According to the Old Testament, for three years, Judah paid taxes to Babylonia until King Jehoiakim decided to stop the payments and went to war with Babylonia. In the 6th century BCE, the Jews were exiled from the Kingdom of Judah to Babylon by Nebuchadnezzar. Nebuchadnezzar and his history would have been mostly lost had it not been preserved by the Jews who wrote scripts regarding their history.

Nebuchadnezzar originally sent his army to Jerusalem because Jehoiakim, king of Judah, had decided to rebel against Babylon and stop paying tribute. King Jehoiakim died and was succeeded by his 18-year-old son, Jehoiachin. The new king surrendered to Nebuchadnezzar and was exiled to Babylon. Nebuchadnezzar appointed Jehoiachin's uncle, Mattaniah, as King of Judea and would change his name to Zedekiah.

Zedekiah then also rebelled against Nebuchadnezzar, causing Nebuchadnezzar to attack and eventually breach the walls of the great city, Jerusalem. Zedekiah escaped but was eventually captured and brought to Nebuchadnezzar. Zedekiah witnessed his sons slaughtered before him and then had his own eyes taken out, and was sent in captivity to Babylon. Zedekiah's treachery would result in Nebuzaradan[2] burning down the Temple in Jerusalem under Nebuchadnezzar's orders, and the Jews would be taken into exile in Babylon.

In Babylon, Nebuchadnezzar selected four Judea boys— Daniel, Hananiah, Mishael and Azariah—for service in the Babylonian royal court. Daniel would stand out, not only for the King but for the Jews whose historical records would exalt him in the book of Daniel. Daniel's legacy came from his ability to help the King with a dream.

It seemed that Nebuchadnezzar had a very disturbing dream, but alas, one the King could not remember. He ordered his wise men and magicians to tell him not only what he had dreamed but what the dream had meant. The King ordered all of them to death if they could not do so. This of course was a very difficult task, to remember the dream of another man, and so most magicians were unable to do so. This led the King to order all of their deaths. Only Daniel would take up the cause and say, "Do not do away with the wise men of Babylon; bring me to the King and I will tell the King the meaning!" (Daniel 2:24)

Daniel told the King of his own dream as opposed to the King's dream. He told Nebuchadnezzar of his dream of a great statue. This statue had a silver breast, brass thighs, iron legs and feet of clay. But the head was gold. The statue would be broken by a simple throw of a stone. The pieces, however, would be swept away by the wind and grow into a great mountain that filled the earth. The gold head, Daniel explained, was Nebuchadnezzar, and the other parts of the statue were the empires that would follow the great empire of Nebuchadnezzar. All of these empires would be swept away by the Kingdom of God, which would be eternal.

Nebuchadnezzar appointed Daniel as governor of Babylon and head of all the wise men in the kingdom. Thus, the story begins with a king who would play both antagonist and protagonist for the Jews, actually lifting them to a position of great power in the city and the kingdom of Babylon. Nebuchadnezzar, according to scripture, was succeeded by his son Belshazzar. It would be during his son's reign that Babylon would fall to the Persians, and thus the beginning of Daniel's prophecy of successive empires that would be swept away, including the empires of Alexander the Great, the Romans and the Persians again.

In the book of Ezra, one can clearly see the social community of Jewish Babylonia. By the 6th century BCE, many of the Jews returned to Israel and began the rebuilding of the second

Temple in Jerusalem. But Babylon still played a major role for the Jews, including in the writing of the Babylonian Talmud. Up until the Islamic Caliphate, Babylonia was a center for Jewish learning.

The Jewish population in Iraq declined during the Mongol period and under Islam in the Middle Ages. The Ottomans were more tolerant of the Jewish people than the Mongols had been. When Britain took over the Ottoman Empire in 1932, Iraq became a nation-state with a constitutional monarchy. In 1958, it became a republic, and Iraqi Jews would play an important role in Iraq's independence; unfortunately, it was a republic in name only, and would be ruled by a series of dictators, the last of which was Saddam Hussein.

The Holocaust by Another Name

After World War I and the fall of the Ottoman Empire, the Hashemite Kingdom of Iraq was founded by Great Britain in 1921. In 1941, at the height of fascism in the world, Rashid Ali, an Iraqi Nazi, overturned the Hashemite Kingdom and implemented, albeit for a short period, fascism in Iraq.

The turning point for the Jews in Iraq was the violent and deadly Farhud, mentioned earlier, which took place between June 1-2, 1941. The pro-Nazi Golden Square Regime and its leader, Rashid Ali al-Kaylani, killed over 180 Jews in two days of violence. It was becoming clear that Jews were being blamed for economic conditions, and the success of some members of their community became the evidence.

The Allied forces quickly moved upon the Iraqi Nazi government in the Anglo-Iraqi War, reestablishing Allied control. But it was clear that short of outside intervention, the racist views of fascism had a core group of support in Iraq. The creation of the State of Israel exacerbated these tensions and ignited anti-Zionist propaganda and conspiracy theories.

In 1948, Israel was declared a state. During this period, Jews around the world understood the backlash to the creation of Israel put many Jews around the world in danger. Most Jews identify with the testament of "Never Again," meaning never again shall we allow ourselves to be victims.

Survivors of the Nazi Holocaust understood how easy it was to misinterpret the perils and potential atrocities of a truly authoritarian government. They understood that it would be impossible to predict potential atrocities at the beginning of a genocide. While one could see signs in the appointment of a dictator, the undermining of free media and the demagogic language that demonizes a group of people, one could still not be certain that such a movement would turn violent and genocidal.

The people who were targets of a genocidal movement could misunderstand the risk of staying in the place that they called home. Those Holocaust survivors understood the victims faced the difficult choice to give up their friends, their money, their property and their homes, or stay and hope for the best. They would have to leave for a place they had never been to, and they would have no money to get there. The survivors understood the difficulties of leaving home, even under the threat of tyrannical governments. These survivors also understood well the dangers of not doing so. And so they put a plan in place to help the victims who would face the backlash of the extended Holocaust.

By 1950 in Iraq, the amount of publicly endorsed hangings of Jewish citizens, mock trials and bombings had risen to a point that Jews around the world knew that help was needed. The Iraqi government reversed an earlier prohibition of Jewish emigration to Israel and passed a one-year duration in which Jews could leave so long as they renounced citizenship. Iraqi leadership found the benefit of such a policy would increase the treasury as the government would take possession of the Jewish property.

American Jews formed the American Joint Distribution Committee[3] and funded Operation Ezra and Nehemiah with four million dollars to provide transport, money and a place to go for Jews in trouble.[4] This would be named after Ezra and Nehemiah, who led the Jewish people out of exile from Babylonia back to their homeland in the 5th century BCE.

Between 1950 and 1952, over 120,000 to 130,000 Iraqi Jews reached Israel during Operation Ezra and Nehemiah. These Jews were airlifted through Iran and Cyprus in one of the most dramatic events of the exile of Jews into Israel. Very few Jewish families remained in Iraq, but young Joseph's family was one of them.

As with Evelyn's story, the power to objectify people creates a justification for unjust actions. As individuals, objectifying people can be very harmful to our relationships and to our mental well-being. But when a demagogue begins to objectify groups of people, the results can be catastrophic to a given order.

The narrative of Saddam Hussein and the Ba'ath Party was that Jews who occupied Iraq were aliens who had invaded the Islamic people. Yet, Jews had been a part of Iraq's history since the early days of Nebuchadnezzar's Babylonian Empire. They contributed wealth, ideas, literature, art and made society richer. They were in no way aliens; they were a part of the Iraqi fabric.

But Saddam and the Ba'ath Party, through relativism such as that promoted by Nietzsche, believed that alternative facts were more important, and the construct that one lived within was determined by the individual telling the story. This theory of relativism can be much better understood by Americans in 2020 after experiencing QAnon, conspiracy theories and the invasion of the Capitol that sprang from the belief in alternative facts. The more powerful the leader who espouses such alternatives, the more the construct is accepted.

The story that Hussein and the Ba'ath Party told was that Jews were alien to Iraqi culture. I spent significant time working with undocumented immigrants from Mexico and Latin America in later years and found it ironic that in many ways their stories mimicked those of my Iraqi parents. These were Americans whose families were indigenous to the Southwest, and in fact, had existed here before Caucasians and Europeans. They have been a significant part of the culture long before the current divide.

I do not want to underestimate the complexity of many of the problems that come with sanctuary and immigration, both legal and otherwise. But I do want to recognize that those problems are not the same as the narrative given to us by politicians who are hoping to obtain a political objective. Their objective is to accumulate power by using these issues to divide us. This is damaging to all immigrants, irrespective of status.

For young Joseph and his family, regardless of the unfairness, the political environment created a necessity for them to escape.

9

TIME FOR ME TO GO HOME
2000—ZANZIBAR

I woke up in sheets that were covered in sweat. I could see the rain outside. The inside of my body was freezing, but the outside of my body was pouring sweat. My skin was on fire.

I could not focus. The night before, I was having problems connecting words to thoughts, but now I was completely delirious. The nervous system that connected my brain to my limbs was not operating correctly. I could not voluntarily move my legs or my arms. My joints cracked and ached in pain from any movement in my body.

This was the first time I ever remember feeling death in my body. I knew that I had caught something while in the tropical jungles of Pemba Island in the waters of the Indian Ocean. I knew that without help quickly, I was not going to survive.

When I left Egypt and the sands where I had begun the practice of my belly dancing, I left for other parts of Africa. I trekked through the jungles of Pemba and explored Lamu Island and Zanzibar. I safaried through the Masai Mara and Lake Nakuru and scuba-dived in the Indian Ocean.

Somewhere along this journey, I had run into mosquitoes that had carried the malaria virus.

For weeks, the delirium lingered. I was helpless. Without the help of friends, I would have died of dehydration or starvation. Even though I had left the rugged underdeveloped terrain and was now in Switzerland, all I can remember is gloom and darkness.

As I recovered, I made a life-changing decision. I was going to return to Vancouver, stay with my aunt Tracy and uncle Salman and focus on higher education. It was the beginning of my journey to become a psychologist.

Vancouver is a beautiful city. It has an urban population whose progressive ideas were formed by a society more focused on the collective than the individualistic United States. Vancouver has a commitment to higher education, and while it has several universities, it has an academic culture in almost any coffee shop.

People there love talking about ideas, science, politics and world affairs, albeit in a traditional Canadian style, where they are careful not to offend.

In my undergraduate years at the University of British Columbia, I focused on psychology and assisted with research on religious intolerance. When doing my master's work in Australia at Flinders University, I wrote my thesis on the pathway of revenge justification and intergroup conflict. Later in my doctoral program in the US, I conducted my research on human rights abuses of undocumented Latinas, along with pioneering psychologists Dr. Louise Baca and Dr. Karen Suyemoto.

My parents' journey had an incredible effect on my sense of justice. Generally, a person who is focused on justice will work in law enforcement, prosecution or defense. But justice for people like my parents rarely comes about from a courtroom or a jail cell, or involves perpetrators suffering a penalty.

The only justice for people like my parents is coming to peace with the multitude of losses and trauma, forging ahead, persevering despite the many obstacles, embracing life and focusing on building their future while not being paralyzed by the past.

The wounds made on my parents by Saddam Hussein and his torturers were so deep that unless you knew them intimately, you would not hear them speak of it. My parents viewed complaining about the lot they had been given in life as being ungrateful. And yet, from knowing them, I knew that their pain was so deep that it left scars. I was compelled by the thought of helping them and others like them cope with that trauma or such unspoken grief.

To truly understand my parents and the pain that they went through, I knew that it was not enough to simply hear the shortened versions of their infrequently told tales. In fact, I was compelled to try to comprehend what happened to them. I believe this drove what became a focus of my education, trying to elucidate the underlying mechanisms of religious intolerance, vengeance and human rights abuses. I sought knowledge from others who had found themselves in similar positions that my parents had experienced during the Ba'ath Party in Iraq. In Israel, I had the opportunity to work for a short time with Palestinian girls. Here, in this small rural town in Gaza, these young women had so much potential. Time had not yet built up the scars that would leave them angry. You could still hear the hope in their voices and see the promise and curiosity in their eyes.

This was very different from what I saw with the undocumented Latinas I worked with in Arizona. Not only did these women tell stories of the brutality of crossing the desert, they were also being taken advantage of by the coyotes (human traffickers). They also suffered from lack of water, unrelenting heat, pain, damage to their feet from the hot sand and blisters from the sun. They spoke about exploitation, extortion and being violently abused. They also witnessed the victimization of others, which included robbery, sexual slavery and rape.

They spoke about enduring human rights abuses by border patrol agents in the desert. They were humiliated and treated like animals, and some were run over with quads. Upon entering into custody, they found it to be no better than the suffering they experienced in crossing. So many of the migrants had consistent stories about abuse from within the detention centers.

Those stories included the panic that happened when border patrol agents set upon them with four-wheel drive vehicles, running people down. They described the agents cursing at them, using slurs, degrading their intellect and race and making an overall effort to dehumanize them.

My understanding of how a fascist government could engage innocent citizens in a quest to suppress people became enlightened. I began to understand that these forces that we hear about, from the Khmer Rouge in Cambodia, Maoism in China and Stalinism in Russia were not born from the isolated characteristics of people in a foreign land, but of human characteristics that could afflict people anywhere. The treatment that these immigrants received was not exactly the same as that of oppressed groups under tyrannical governments; however, the origin of their mistreatment was the same: dehumanization. And I feel like it gave me a better understanding of what had happened to my parents.

During this time, I never gave up my love of belly dancing. I discovered an ability to find joy and light through my art that allowed me to stay connected to people I might not have otherwise. Practicing belly dancing, working on human rights abuses with immigrants, building friends in the Arab community and honing my linguistic and cultural understanding of the Arabic community all laid the path for beginning to understand the layers of subcultures that exist in any society. It eventually led me to the psychological work that I do in clinical and forensic settings through having a deeper appreciation of the variety of cultures and contextual factors in the Middle East. It also led me to develop expertise in the cultural formulations of individuals within the criminal justice system.

10

WHEN HOME DISAPPEARS

1973—BAGHDAD, IRAQ

Leaving Iraq was not an easy decision for any family to make. They had to be willing to walk away from everything they had spent their lifetimes accumulating—not just money, property and businesses, but family, friends and a way of life. The fear of leaving was almost overpowering. And while the living conditions in Iraq had become terrible, there was always a hope that the oppression, terror and murder would end. But the 1969 hangings would change that feeling, which is exactly what they were designed to do.

When young Joseph returned home from the hangings, he rushed in to tell the family what he had seen. It was evident from their furrowed brows and tight lips that they were deeply stressed by the day's events. Joseph's uncle[1] had spent his life amassing large sums of land. That land was farmed along the Tigris and Euphrates Rivers, as it had been for centuries, and was still fertile ground.

Aside from farms, he also used the land to create other businesses like car dealerships. He understood that as it was becoming more difficult for Jews to own land, being in business was a good alternative. Young Joseph's entire family worked for his uncle.

Success has 1,000 enemies, and envy was one of the enemies of the Bashah farmers. History has shown that when an economy suffers and people lose something they once had, a reliable political tactic is to blame minorities, immigrants or the wealthy for that loss. It creates a scapegoat, telling people the reason they are suffering is "those people over there."

In 1972, Hussein was not yet in full charge of the Ba'ath Party. His role under his cousin, who was in charge, was security, and that gave him the power to imprison, terrorize and murder other Iraqis. In Iraq, the Ba'ath Party and Hussein had found the ability to blame a group that encompassed all three common scapegoats: minorities, immigrants and the wealthy.

Even though the Jewish population could trace their heritage in Iraq back further than the Islamic population, they were still seen as immigrants, outsiders who had come from somewhere else and did not belong. The hard-working nature and entrepreneurial spirit of some Jewish families had been exploited for political purposes and calculated to appeal to the desires and prejudices of a collective. Iraqi politicians began to demagogue the Jews by manipulating the narrative of how Jews had prospered unfairly and at the expense of other Iraqis. With Israel being a newly formed state, they could argue how Zionism was really a secret cabal designed to harm Muslims.

Joseph's uncle became one of these examples. After seizing his land and taking his money, Uncle Bashah was shamed on television and charged with being a spy for Israel. His hair was shaved off to further dehumanize, humiliate and publicly shame him, and he was threatened with death. They released him the same day, knowing he would escape Iraq, abandon his land, farm and real estate and leave behind all of his goods to be sequestered by the government. If he did not, he would die.

Joseph's uncle acted accordingly and left that day for Iran, and later, Israel.

The Bashah family was terrified as well as stressed about financially supporting themselves. They knew they had to get out of Iraq. It was long past time to leave behind everything they had ever known. They decided that Joseph and his younger two brothers would go first. The family decided to utilize the underground railroad, which had been established over the past two decades of Jewish exile from Iraq. This wasn't always the safest route because it was organized both by people who truly cared and those who only wanted to profit, but it was their best bet.

The first step was to get the brothers from Baghdad to Mosul. Joseph and his two brothers took the train there, then went on by taxi to the city of Erbil. Erbil could date its inhabitants back to the early settlement of 4,000 BCE and the Semitic-speaking kingdom of Ebla in 2,300 BCE.[2] It became the capital of the Kurdistan region. It was Kurds who helped the brothers escape into a more Jewish-friendly country, Iran, in 1972. Eventually, the Islamic Revolution would catch up to Iran, but for that period of time, it was run by the Shah of Iran, who was more friendly to the Jews.

When the Bashah brothers arrived in Erbil, Iraq, they met a group of Kurds. These Kurds were paid to get the brothers through the mountains and into Iran. They were business people but compassionate to the cause, as they were also a victimized group.

Kurds are the largest ethnic minority persecuted in Middle Eastern countries, and yet most are Muslims. They were known as awesome fighters and had no problem defying the local government, especially if they could be paid for doing so. These Kurds were happy to smuggle the Bashah brothers across the border.

The history of the Kurdish people and their ethnic purity is tied to the Kurdish mountains. Persians, Alexander the Great, Muslims in the 7th century, Turks in the 11th, Mongols in the 13th, Persians again and the Ottomans all tried to conquer and occupy the Kurdish land and its people. The land the Kurds occupied was one of the crossroads of the Middle East that could connect disparate areas that an empire might want to connect. And the Kurds, over and again, had been a thorn to many great empires.

With the fall of the Ottoman Empire after World War I, the British and French divided the Middle East into nation-states to serve their colonial interests. After hundreds of years under Ottoman control, Syria and Mesopotamia were separated into five nation-states. Syria and Lebanon were under French control and Palestine, Jordan and Iraq, including Mosul Province, were under British control.

By the time the British and French controlled Kurdish lands, the Kurds had established themselves as Kurdish nationalists. Kurds had converted to Muslims after the Arab invasion. They had shifted between Sunni Muslims and Shiite Muslims depending upon who the conquering government was, as more of a political statement than a deep devout dogma. But the one dogma that Kurds held onto was their role as freedom fighters, and in 1970s Iraq, they were the Kurdish Democratic Party (KDP).[3]

The mountains saved the Kurdish people from rape, murder and genocide many times over. They knew how to hide and survive there. These rugged mountains allowed the Kurds to retain their distinct ethnic identity. Their willingness to fight for their independence often made them an enemy of occupying regimes, so the Kurds were no friends to the Iraqi government. And although they had no particular allegiance to the Iraqi Jews either, countering the government that oppressed them and engaging in human smuggling was good politics and good business. Protecting their paying customers was important for more business, and this is what the Bashah boys relied on to escape Iraq.

When night came, the brothers heard a truck driving up the dirt road. Once it arrived, they were led back to the canvas-covered truck bed. The flap was opened, revealing their traveling companions: mules. The stench was potent, but the mules would prove an invaluable part of their escape. For now, the boys were loaded into the back of the truck with the animals and driven to a trail outside of town.

It was a moonless night, which gave them the cover of complete darkness. However, it made the trail less visible and the mules all the more important. The boys, along with other Jews who were being smuggled out, were offloaded from the truck. As the boys mounted their animals, they wondered if these Kurds might turn them over to Iraqi authorities or hold them for ransom.

The Kurds worked in silence. They hooked the mules by rope to one another. Then one Kurd got in front and began to lead them into the dark, narrow pass. The group of 10 mules began the trek across the treacherous but Kurdish-dominated Qandil Mountains.

The Qandil Mountains are known for their extremely rugged terrain and are very difficult to cross. But these mountains lie on the border of Iran. There was no security or border crossing to stop the Kurds from leading these young Jewish boys across to freedom.

Riding the mule quickly became uncomfortable, and Joseph asked one of the Kurds if he and his brothers could walk instead. As the mules headed into the treacherous mountains, the answer became self-evident. The trails were narrow and steep, the night was dark, and as Joseph looked over the edge, he saw only a bottomless abyss.

Joseph leaned forward to take the pressure off his bottom. The melting snow created a cool breeze. Their family and the home they had known their entire lives was behind them. In front of them, all that existed now was hope.

As the mules came down off the mountain, Joseph could see a camp below. They approached a gated entrance that was not much more than a light and a parking lot. Kurds armed with AK-47s walked to the entrance.

The boys and other refugees got off the mules and walked across the border. They were met by another big truck that picked them up to transport them to a small hotel. The border town was run down and primitive, where homes were nothing more than mud huts. Goats walked freely on the dirt streets.

At the hotel, there were 30 other Iraqi Jews. They had the faces of men and women who had lost everything, yet maybe they had gained all that really mattered. The next stop was Tehran, which was 14 hours away.

In 1970, the Shah of Iran was a friend of the United States and gave exiled Iraqi Jews sanctuary. The Islamic Revolution had not yet transpired, and Tehran was a very modernized city. Tehran was developed with elegant shops and gathering places. It was a nice place to spend the next two weeks while they waited to be flown into Israel and processed as Israeli citizens. When the Israeli consulate met them, they felt like they were going to a new home.

It was the thought of a new life that moved them forward.

Certainly, the lessons of Joseph's life in Iraq are very similar to Evelyn's. But the one additional lesson is one I am hesitant to give. In all of my experience with all of my clients, I have found one of the keys to their success is the ability to be focused, disciplined, persistent and understand that happiness is an inside job. Quite often people abandon their marriage or their family or their home in pursuit of happiness or self-gratification, only to find the ability to gain it was always inside of them.

But Joseph's and Evelyn's lives, and what happened to their families, parents and their people, teaches us that every so often, the events transpiring around you are much bigger than you are. When you are swept up in these moments of history where the forces of light and darkness are magnified, sometimes the only choice is to leave behind all that you know and start a new beginning. This is difficult to understand for many people who have just simply never personally experienced such horrific and historical events. But what happened with Saddam Hussein is certainly not unique. It has been repeated with despots like Joseph Stalin, Ida Amin, Pol Pot, Slobodan Milošević and the list continues. In these circumstances, you cannot beat history. And it seems that your only choice is to leave everything you know behind.

My maternal aunt Ferial acted bravely to do what she could to save her father. When she arrived with her husband in Israel, she begged Golda Meir to go to Baghdad to save her imprisoned father and the remainder of her family. Meir scoffed at her and asked, "Why did they remain in Iraq?" Meir knew that what was happening with Hussein was no different from what had occurred with Hitler two generations prior. It seemed incredible to her that Jews who had witnessed the Holocaust could not see that it could happen again. The slogan of Israel, "Never Again," has many intended impacts on the Jewish psyche. At least a part of it is to remind us that this threat is something we have lived with for thousands of years, and the only way to maintain the survival of the Jewish people is to never forget how it happened and never become complacent so that it could be attempted again.

I often wonder if I had been born in Iraq how different my life and I would be. Would my free-spirited nature have been tamed? Would my quest for truth, knowledge and understanding have been deprived? Would I have been pacified to accept the life I was born into? There is no way to be sure that I would still be the same human I am today. And I imagine that for my family, there was no way for them to have survived so long as they hung onto their past. Looking back, it's obvious that there was only one answer: if you were Jewish, you needed to leave it all behind.

11

AN AMERICAN ISLAMIC RADICALIZATION
2019—AN UNDISCLOSED TYPICAL NEIGHBORHOOD IN AMERICA

A young teenage boy, Sal, stood on a street corner near the gas station where an armed robbery had occurred just days prior. He was wearing open-toed sandals, shorts, a dark sweatshirt with a hood covering his head and a small black backpack. He stood in the street taunting a police officer to shoot him. It was an evening not unlike any other. The sky was clear and the moon was full, illuminating the streets. The air was chill and crisp. A streetlight lit the area where Sal and the officer stood.

The police officer yelled for Sal to raise his hands. Sal resisted the orders and, keeping his hands in his pockets, took another step toward the officer. While Sal was not observably hostile or violent, he knew the consequences of his actions. Approaching the officer in this way was an attempt at "suicide by cop." He was determined to sacrifice himself as a martyr for his ideology. Sal had no weapon, and as he moved forward, he recited, "*Allahu Akbar!*", a phrase meaning "God is most great" used by Muslims in prayers and as a general declaration of faith. But to Sal, this was a pledge to radical Islam. He saw no other way to regain his honor and identity than to confront what he viewed as infidels in a corrupt Americanized society. He wanted to die for this cause, and he truly believed his faith beckoned him to do so.

Sal was born in the United States. His father immigrated in search of opportunity, education and tranquility from his war-ridden country and met Sal's mother in the US. Sal's extended family were affluent, well-educated and working professionals for the Pakistani government with respectable jobs in their home country. His parents never suspected the events that were about to unfold for their son.

Sal grew up aligning with American ideals, but as an Arab Muslim during the years following 9/11, he found himself isolated at his school and among his peers. He was looking for a sense of belonging, a community and the opportunity to create meaning and purpose in his life. He also wanted to uphold his family's honor. He was lost, isolated and searching for a greater cause.

In his search for himself and an identity, he found Muslim social connections online. They understood him and spoke of how they had encountered the same type of covert and overt discrimination. They connected to him by talking about who they were and the proud heritage they came from. It was easy to find like-minded individuals online. Unfortunately, one of those like minds that he found linked him to a radical organization. Young Sal would have no way of knowing that this person was a radical Islamic recruiter who wanted to indoctrinate him into a life of martyrdom and violence.

Sal, whose character was historically nonviolent, meek and anxiety-prone by nature, contacted law enforcement and made threats to damage federal buildings and the people inside of them.

Whatever comments he provided were a sufficient threat for an officer to be called out to the scene.

The officer who arrived did not want to harm the young

man. Yet, for the officer, life and death decisions had to be made instinctively and without hesitation. He was trained to fire if someone provided cause. But in an ambiguous situation like this, that decision wasn't easy or instant.

The officer hesitated one second longer in hopes that Sal would comply with his commands. But when Sal openly continued his threats, the officer commanded Sal one final time to get down on the ground. Sal did not obey. As Sal charged forward, the officer pulled the trigger and shot Sal in the leg.

Sal was sent into a criminal justice system that has no understanding of how to deal with deradicalization. Instead, it is a system designed with a win-or-lose construct that doesn't know what to do with someone like Sal. Releasing him was not an option. His careless disregard for his life and the life of others showed that he remained a danger to society. Sal's social media revealed detailed plans, motives and coaching by extreme religious leaders. The FBI immediately began an investigation and obtained a search warrant to seize his computers, electronic devices and potential equipment to be used in an attack on US soil. All of this was a surprise to his parents, who had not known of Sal's declining mental and behavioral health over the months leading up to his arrest. The incident brought shame to their family, not honor.

For the sake of preserving confidentiality, Sal is a fictitious name and much of the case-related information has been combined from numerous similar cases. Facts have been altered so as not to identify confidential information about the forensic cases I've been involved in.

According to recent data from the International Center for Counter-Terrorism at the Hague, homegrown jihadists represent a very small portion of Muslims.[1] While it is difficult to determine how many Arab Americans become radicalized, studies show that homegrown jihadists may total dozens to a few hundred converts in any given year, which represents a small number in any Western democracy.[2] Sal could represent any number of young Arab-American, Muslim boys, not as homegrown jihadists, but instead those who are at the greatest risk of radicalization because of their isolation, marginalization and discrimination based on religion and race. All of which makes them vulnerable to being preyed upon by recruiters for radicalization.

Among other studies, the Center for Strategic and International Studies points out that right-wing extremists pose the biggest threat to the United States based on terrorism and fatalities.[3]

Sal came from a respected family that was not marginalized. But for Sal, his educational experience resulted in alienation from other students and failure academically. Within radical websites, he was able to find a place where he could excel and where others who were either like him or understood how to take advantage of him fed his need for praise, acceptance, value and self-worth.

We are seeing with increased regularity the need for psychologists who can help deprogram young people who are being indoctrinated into religious extremism by radical conspiracy theorists and ideological cults. In many ways, Western democracy is being bombarded with cult-like environments that are radicalizing people into violence. Alas, this is not isolated to the ideologies of radical Islam. We are seeing the same from other groups, and right-wing national groups are considered to be the biggest threat of domestic terrorism.

Radicalized websites—whether from ISIS and Al Qaeda or QAnon and Proud Boys—all utilize similar tactics to indoctrinate their members. First, they target people who feel that they have been aggrieved—for example, those suffering economically or feeling discarded by society's changing social norms. Often, when someone files bankruptcy, loses their job or is hit with bills that they cannot pay—or they have become the object of ridicule, scorn or isolation from societal norms—they begin to feel disconnected from society and even resentful toward it for rejecting them. These individuals will find themselves alone, angry and hurt and begin to look for other like-minded people.

Ideological obsession is certainly not isolated to the right. In the 1960s, radical left-wing groups were much bigger than the right. George Washington University provides a program on both violent and non-violent extremism. In November of 2021, they released a study titled "Anarchist/Left-Wing Violent Extremism in America: Trends in Radicalization, Recruitment, and Mobilization." The US government defines anarchist violent extremists as domestic violent extremists who oppose all forms of capitalism, corporate globalization and governing institutions. The definition includes anarchists holding other left-wing violent ideologies who violate the law or otherwise meet the definitions of domestic terrorism.[4] The study showed a history of violence but only isolated incidents of violence over the last few years. Nonetheless, these groups are still considered to be a threat.

On the right, we see the story on the nightly news. The good news is that in 2021, few deaths occurred from anti-government white nationalists or other right-wing organizations, unlike the 2018 Pittsburgh synagogue shooting or the 2019 El Paso Walmart attack. The bad news is that violent rhetoric is becoming normalized.[5] According to one poll, 30 percent of Republicans agreed with the statement that "things have gotten so far off track we may have to resort to violence to save our country."[6]

Threats from racially motivated groups are becoming a greater focus of the US Department of Justice.[7] The raid on the United States Capitol by groups like the Oath Keepers and the Proud Boys was largely driven by race. These groups, along with more elaborate conspiracy movements like QAnon, create a pathway and quick solution to an explosive problem that individuals feel they have no control over or power to influence. The solutions are usually simple and offer an opportunity to externalize the blame and deny oneself of any responsibility for the problem. The characterological makeup of such individuals is that they feel stigmatized, rejected, angry and marginalized. An opportunity to displace the blame externally offers relief and egoistic self-preservation. An added benefit for these individuals is the offer of hope for something better, which is often a promise by leaders in exchange for full devotion and sacrifice for the cause. For those looking for belonging, purpose and a sense of self-worth, this promise is seductive. The ideology becomes an obsession reflected in all that they say, do and think about.

The ideological addiction of these true believers influences them to join these groups without hesitation, leading them to believe the wild conspiracy theories over reality. Over time, it becomes critical to their construct that what they believe defies logic or reasoning. QAnon has led millions to believe that pedophiles control the government, and that some deep state agent, "Q," delivers information to recruits in cryptic phrases designed to create speculation that the followers will be protected by Donald Trump himself.

Discerning Trump's motivation for all this is beyond the scope of what we want this book to be focused on. From a psychological view, Donald Trump almost undoubtedly was a victim of severe trauma in his life. While acclaimed psychologists have suggested Trump has Narcissistic Personality Disorder,[8] and his niece Mary Trump spoke about his abandonment by his mother and his father's sadistic emotional abuse, they have suggested that Trump has a psychological inability to deal with failure and accountability. But for his supporters, this may be hard to acknowledge, and is perhaps inconsequential to their fundamental belief system. For example, many of the participants of the Capitol insurrection were clearly driven by motives that extended beyond their support of Trump. Some had existing addictions to a radical ideology led by Stuart Rhodes, a Yale-educated lawyer who launched the Oath Keepers on April 19th, 2009, long before Trump was even considered as a candidate for president. According to his defense regarding his role in the Capitol riots, Stuart Rhodes urged the president to invoke the 1807 Insurrection Act, which, in his opinion, gave the president the right to call up a militia. That militia, according to Rhodes's plan, would be the Oath Keepers and the other groups at the Capitol that day. Invoking that act would empower him and his group the right to take arms into the Capitol.

The Insurrection Act began with Aaron Burr, who in 1806 had allegedly tried to start a rebellion in the American Southwest. Rhodes and others had convinced a great many people that the President would issue such an order. Participants of the Capitol riots, who put themselves in danger, expressed shock when the president did not implement the Insurrection Act in their defense.

The Capitol insurrection was like an exaggerated version of Pizzagate, where an armed gunman entered a pizza parlor based on information furnished by the conspiracy site Info-Wars that a group of pedophiles led by Hillary Clinton kept children imprisoned in the basement there. The gunman surrendered himself and his assault weapon when he realized that no basement existed and he had been duped.

For groups like the Oath Keepers, it seems clear to us that the goal of the Capitol insurrection was to overthrow democracy itself, as the racist objectives of the Oath Keepers are all but impossible to achieve in an environment where the majority rules. But many of the participants said they believed that they were there to save the integrity of elections. They could not fully appreciate the severity of the consequences of their actions and that they had actually participated in an egregious offense towards disrupting free elections. They did not openly recognize the destructive nature of their hostilities toward the Constitution or the rule of law because their perceptions and belief systems involved a distorted reality.

Ultimately they were there because an ideological leader exploited an opportunity to be their savior in exchange for their agency. Like Sal, they had bought into a paradigm that manipulated them through the scarcity mindset that everything was being robbed from them, with a very simple message: scapegoat, promise and solution.

Our neurocognitive function works in such a way that amplifying emotional reasoning hijacks the neocortex from employing logical reason, attention, insight, impulse control and judgment. The Capitol rioters may have been driven by fear of being replaced, made irrelevant or losing what little they felt they had. The ideology not only made them feel good about themselves, but it also included them in a group membership that enhanced a sense of belonging and commitment to a greater cause.

They benefited from being part of a group, a group that made them feel important, powerful and in control. It gave them a status that made them part of something bigger and promoted their self-esteem. And even though their actions dramatically increased the chance they would lose their freedom to a tyrant, they were willing to give that up. They believed this because for months if not years, their perceptions of reality were being distorted. They were still competent for their actions, yet like Sal, they had long ago lost their sense of agency. They were afflicted with an addictive ideology.

For these individuals, many started out by simply doing a web search and then, through algorithms that promote the echo chamber, they became flooded with like-minded ideas, conspiracies and ideologies. This echo chamber of falsehoods and alternative realities became legitimized by the words and actions of the President of the United States. These two factors together are unprecedented in history.

The United States borrowed from antiquity many of the great concepts that make up our democratic republic. The Senate, commander in chief, Congress, the judiciary, the rule of law and even rights and liberties were all borrowed from antiquity. The one unique thing about American democracy was the peaceful transfer of power. From 1791 until 2021, that had gone off almost without a hitch.

Before the 2020 election took place, we began to see erosion at a very high level of our faith in the American democratic system. From the 2000 election, the *Bush v. Gore* landmark decision of the United States Supreme Court settled a recount dispute and sowed doubt on the court and the election system. In 2018, Stacey Abrams's unwillingness to concede the Georgia governor's race cast doubt to her supporters on the legitimacy of elections. Our electoral system was already showing the wear of the divisions in the US.

President Trump foreshadowed his actions by telling Americans that, in fact, if he were to lose for any reason, it could only happen because of a fraudulent election. From Election Day to January 6th, 2021, the president would bash the free election system, intimidate Republican secretaries of state and demonize Republican governors who would not support changing the outcome. All of this was amplified by radical websites convincing their followers that judgment day had come.

On Election Day, polling indicated that even a majority of Republicans, while deeply disappointed in the results, had faith that the election was fair and that the results were accurate and factual. Day by day, as the disinformation campaign persisted, delivered by the highest elected official in the land, it was like watching a nuclear countdown take place in our free election system. And on January 6th, we moved from DEFCON 5 to DEFCON 1.

This was an intentional and premeditated attack on the foundation of our American system. We watched this cultish practice take place in front of our eyes on television. We listened as a percentage of our friends and family who we care about actually bought into the abandonment of American principles for the possibility, hope and promise of something better, in exchange for their agency.

If you can understand what happened on that frightful day of January 6th, when a group of true believers stormed the Capitol and threatened to take the lives of democratically elected officials, then you should also be able to understand what happens within radicalized Islamic organizations or authoritarian governments. People who are disenfranchised, who believe that they have been lied to or that they do not fit in, find a cause to belong to and people of like minds to associate with. Social media platforms that were supposed to connect us and help us find friends instead promoted vast division and isolation. The consequence of this is a public that feels more divided than ever and individuals who mistake the shared hatred they find online as a substitute for real and meaningful connection.

Groups who are trying to condition their followers have to start by destroying the reality that they know. This gives them an alternative view of the facts, building for them a new history and narrative that allows them to feel that they are a part of something bigger, and that they are legitimate, powerful and justified. The next step is to influence others that their dogma is accurate and superior to bolster their worldview and belief system. In such cases, democracy is the enemy of dogma. Autocracy is preferred over democratic republics. What is truly at stake with all of these organizations is whether the idea of the individual or the freedoms allocated to them through the Declaration of Independence can survive.

But the challenge is that the democratic republic, whose constitution provides for the protection of those individuals, can also provide the very framework used by extremists to over-throw democratic rule and implement what many of us would call a dystopian future. This is not an easy sociopolitical impasse for us to confront.

We must look at radicalization holistically and seek to not only understand the threat it poses to Western democracy, but also the underlying root cause of such ideologies—and further, to elucidate the tactics and strategies that can be successful in deprogramming them.

The Rand Study from 2010[9] on the radicalization of reli-gious organizations gave interesting and thoughtful ideas on solving this dilemma. They also gave different solutions that existed in places like Yemen and Saudi Arabia, where civil rights were not expected, versus the types of solutions that exist in places like France and the United States, where liberties are guaranteed through the rule of law and are part of the social fabric.

Significant debate exists on whether the messianic leader comes first or the movement comes first. This binary choice is misguided. In fact, they feed into one another.

Arguably, the genesis of the raid on the Capitol began in 2008, also termed the Great Recession. An American billionaire investor and hedge fund manager, Ray Dalio, describes in his book *Principles for Dealing with the Changing World Order: Why Nations Succeed and Fail* that the public can be separated into what he calls the "asset class" and "working class." During the Great Recession, both suffered incredible setbacks, but the asset class recovered much quicker than the wage class. Since 2008, business income, corporate values and real estate values, all part of the asset class, have more than recovered from their losses in 2008. Wages, however, have remained constant and in many ways, as of the writing of this book, have not recovered from their pre-2008 levels. This not only creates a greater separation between the wealthy and lower income class, but it also creates stress amongst people who have found themselves laid off and oftentimes deployed into jobs without pensions and that pay significantly lower wages than their fathers or mothers earned before them. This is not the majority of Americans, but there is still a significant portion who suffered this fate.

Other parts of this coalition would be the Americans who had suffered from de-industrialization, specifically in the Northeast. Steel mills, coal mines and closed factories littered much of this area—and what was called the Blue Wall, a democratic enclave, was eroding.

Many white working-class people (mostly men) lost their jobs. Average families, who are not part of any hard-right nationalist groups, were feeling the pressure. This was all exacerbated by the nightly news and social media echo chambers.

Those groups of people were ripe for the picking, buying into theories that affirmative action, political correctness and woke culture were taking their livelihoods away. And the leader would feed them with the belief they had been aggrieved by the "elites."

Similar to the 2008 event, which caused economic disparity, 9/11 created xenophobia and a fear of Muslims in the United States. The flip side of that paranoia is that the people who received both micro and macro aggressions and discrimination were marginalized and treated as outsiders.

The first step towards recovery is recognizing you have a problem. It then becomes important to not exacerbate the problem by objectifying those citizens who are being affected by the current dogma on either side. Understanding the cause is important to finding solutions. But those solutions must come not only, as the Rand report indicated,[10] by making it more costly to belong to those organizations via the criminal justice system, but also by how the person is treated after the offense. The only answer to the darkness is light. America was founded on optimism and hope, and we need to embrace those principles now more than ever.

The republic requires that we negotiate to find a compromise, and compromise requires citizens to engage with those who believe they are gaining more than they are losing. We are constantly adjusting on issues that pertain to taxes, Social Security, education, human rights, civil rights and equal rights. That compromise comes through legislation. But if Americans lose the belief that America and its constitution are not worth upholding, then compromise becomes impossible. It is important to all groups that we build pride in who we are, or we will lose what valuable assets we have.

It is not just nationalists or radical Islamists who are addicted to ideology. We are seeing many people in both political parties who place their allegiance to the party above their allegiance to the country. They buy so deeply into being a Republican or being a Democrat that it supersedes being an American. They are so partisan that they take to Facebook to insult and demonize others who they disagree with. They abandon not only decency but often members of their own family who they disagree with. They too are addicted to their ideology.

The Rand study[11] points out that amongst the Americans who are being radicalized into Islamic organizations, the solutions should start by looking at the underlying conditions. Finding ways to connect to these young people through their spiritual leaders, their families, their friends and community leaders are essential. This gives them a sense of belonging, a sense of purpose, and that being an American is something worthy indeed. This is no less what we need to do for individuals who have become addicted to any ideology.

From a psychological standpoint, it was clear that hope had run out for Omar's ability to modify his behavior. But with someone like young Sal, there are alternative solutions to incarceration. In fact, incarceration often leads to greater radicalization as well as providing a greater criminal skill set. From a psychological perspective, threat and risk management assessment informs the level and need for appropriate intervention, psychiatric stabilization, limited access to means of inciting violence, limited access to social media and extremist online sites and a secure level of containment. However, connecting him with his family, the community and his spiritual leaders through a process that is monitored would provide the greatest level of hope for someone like Sal to be deprogrammed and live a fulfilling life as a contributing citizen of worth and value.

Ideology has a way of trying to radicalize all of us. Each of us as individuals have a responsibility to keep ourselves from being radicalized by an Information Age bent on telling us that doom is at our door. Political parties, politicians and news media are biased in influencing our opinions, time and choices through a process of appropriating our agency. We also have to learn our role as citizens to help leave behind something that was as good or better than what we inherited. We have created aspirational ideals to help navigate these challenges.

The Flight of the Prisoners by James Tissot (1896), depicting the exile of the Jews from Canaan to Babylon.

Daniel interprets Nebuchadezzar's Dream by W.A. Spicer (1917).

Daniel in the Lions' Den by Sir Peter Paul Rubens (1614). After rising to high office, Daniel faces the jealousy of non-Jews toward successful Jews and, for holding his faith, is fed to lions. But the story concludes with divine deliverance and a king who confesses the greatness of the God of the Jews and issues an edict of royal protection.

Image from *Our Day in the Light of Prophecy and Providence*, written by William Ambrose Spicer (1921). Depicts the reconstruction of Jerusalem by Cyrus, Darius and Xerxes. Initially, around 50,000 Jews made aliyah to the Land of Judah following the decree of Cyrus as described in the Book of Ezra, whereas most remained in Babylon.

Entry of Alexander into Babylon by Charles Le Brun (1619).

The Siege and Destruction of Jerusalem by the Romans under the Command of Titus, C.E. 70 by David Roberts (1850). When the Romans destroyed Jerusalem, Baghdad again became the center for Judaism.

Harun al-Rashid (r. 786–809) receiving a delegation sent by Charlemagne at his court in Baghdad by German painter Julius Köckert (1864). Islam comes to Baghdad. The city of Baghdad was built in the 8th century and became the primary cultural center of the Muslim world under the Abbasid Caliphate.

Illustration depicting the conquest of Baghdad by the Mongols from a 14th century edition of *Jami' al-tawarikh*, a work of literature written by Rashid al-Din Hamadani (1247–1318).

Ottoman Surrender of Jerusalem Restored by Lewis Larsson (1917). Depicts the Ottoman Mayor of Jerusalem surrendering to the British. The Ottomon Empire lasted from 1534-1920, with an interlude of autonomy under the Mamluk Dynasty of Iraq from 1704-1831.

Photograph of Sir Frederick Stanley Maude leading the Indian Army into Baghdad (1917). At the end of WWI, the British took back control of Iraq.

Photograph of Salah al-Din al-Sabbagh, the Golden Square leader and nationalist who worked with the Nazis on a coup (1930).

Photograph taken during the Farhud, the mass killing of Jews in Iraq (1941).

Photograph depicting the mass grave of Farhud victims (1941). Taken from a page of the book *Iraq*, edited by Haim Saadoun and published by the Ministry of Education and the Ben-Zvi Institute.

A portrait of Faisal II, the last king of Iraq, who reigned from April 1939-July 1958.

Nuri al-Saeed, Prime Minster of Iraq from 1930–1932.

Photograph of Abd al-Karim Qasim and Abd al-Salam, leaders of the July 14th revolution that overthrew the Iraqi monarchy in 1958.

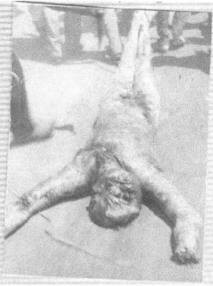

الباشا نوري السعيد مسحولا   الوصي عبد الاله معلقا ومقطع
بسكاكين الشاورما

Photo from 1958 of the mutilated corpses of Prince 'Abd al-Ilah of Hejaz (left) and
Prime Minster Nuri al-Saeed (right). The text in Arabic reads: "Prince 'Abd al-Ilah
hung and cut up by shawarma knives, Pasha Nuri al-Saeed pulled around."

Saddam Hussein and the Ba'ath Party student cell in Cairo between 1959–1963.

Joseph's family when he was a boy; Joseph is on the right with his mother Madeleine Basha and brother.

Joseph's family when he was a boy; Joseph is on the upper right with his two brothers and his father, Naji Ibrahim Basha.

Ezoury Menashi Moshe Shamash and Aziza Leoni Shamash.

Ezoury's family with Evelyn as a girl; Evelyn is in the front on the lower left side.

Ezoury and his family swimming together in the Tigris River.

Ezoury swimming with his son in the Tigris River.

Claire's henna party just prior to Ezoury's disappearance.

Sabah Haim and David Hazaquiel, both Jewish businessmen, after being hanged in Baghdad, Iraq on January 27, 1969 for accusations of being Israeli spies.

Immigrants from Iraq leaving Lod Airport on their way to ma'abara (immigrant and refugee absorption camps in Israel).

Photograph of three Kurdish Jewish family members in the Kurdish mountains in northern Iraq (1905). The Kurdish mountains have jagged and irregular peaks, nearly all of which are taller than 8,000 feet and remain snow-capped for six months of the year.

Joseph with Bedouins.

Joseph in the Israeli Army.

Joseph stationed in Sinai during wartime (1967).

Photograph of Israeli Air Force Mirage IIICJ 158 at the Israeli Air Force Museum in Hatzerim bearing the markings of 13 kills and the colors of the 101 Squadron, similar planes to the ones that Joseph guarded, taken by Oren Rozen (2010).

Photograph taken by the Israel Defense Forces of Israeli tanks crossing the Suez Canal during the Yom Kippur War, where Joseph visited to pick up a car (1973).

Joseph praying at the Wailing Wall in Jerusalem.

Joseph and Evelyn's wedding.

Emily bellydancing in an authentic, handmade bedlah decorated with gold and silver coins.

PART II

THE SEVEN IDEALS OF CITIZENSHIP

INTRODUCTION TO THE SEVEN
IDEALS OF CITIZENSHIP

S ociety based on the individual has always been a challenge.

In 1923, Adolf Hitler sat in a prison cell following his failed Beer Hall Putsch in Munich. Along with Albert Spears, he dedicated five years to writing the two volumes of *Mein Kampf*. In March of 1940, British author George Orwell translated an uncensored version of the book for the *New English Weekly*. He observed that Hitler's book only offered visions struggle, danger and death, and that it had brought all of Germany to its feet. In 1949, Orwell would be inspired, terrified by the vision he read in Hitler's book, to write the dystopian novel *1984*.

But Hitler had offered more than just struggle, danger and death. He was promising a strong Germany, and he gave a complete vision of what that might look like. He gave the reader a scapegoat for why they had failed to accomplish this greatness. Among other things, he mapped out his vision for the role of the state in promoting propaganda that would serve the interest of the *Volk*. In his book, Hitler outlined the role of the German citizen, and how art, music, architecture and news should all serve as a means of propaganda for the state.

It was a pure collectivist vision of the role between the citizen and the government, with the government holding the role of ensuring the success of the German people. His vision included the government holding the role of defining the perfect citizen, providing socialism to give German individuals economic certainty, nationalism to give them military certainty and controlling all propaganda to stop any group from subverting what was in the best interest of the greater good.

It is a tidy sale. "Put me in power," says the despot, "and I will take care of the rest." Throughout history, liberty has been sacrificed for such promises, and in its place, great atrocities have been committed.

This is not what is being sold to you in the American Constitution. Through this document, our social contract, we are buying into the rights and obligations of both the government and its people. Government, according to the first seven articles, was given the right to establish commerce, a military, a congress to write laws, an executive branch to enforce them and courts to interpret the laws and their constitutionality. But the Bill of Rights is the government's obligation to the people.

While the government has accomplished many great things, including building bridges, roads, schools, fighting fires and even putting a man on the moon, the greatest thing our government ever did was to put the rights of the individual over itself. From our prosperity to moving human progress faster and further than any other nation in history, it is this focus on the individual that has made us different.

But that focus on the individual comes with costs. It requires an overwhelming majority of citizens to be willing to be responsible for their obligations. The obligation to pay our taxes, support the outcome of elections and to push for what we believe in legislatively while understanding that we only hold ourselves together through compromises between people who don't necessarily agree with one another. Our obligations as citizens are necessary to make a government of the people, by the people and for the people work.

As the authors, a psychologist and a politician, we both find that no factor matters more to the individual or our collective than people understanding their responsibilities. Each responsibility plays an important role in maintaining our sense of agency. A sense of agency is crucial to fulfill a life of meaning—to create, to love, to innovate and be optimistic. And in turn, owning our sense of agency is important to preserving a republic based on the individual.

For the individual to flourish, they need to be a bit of an idealist. Idealism gets a bad name, based on the notion that it sounds indifferent to realism. Plato spoke about this centuries ago, that the ideal exists in our heads and that what we have here on Earth is merely the representation of those ideals. But we must have an idea of the characteristics that are important to us.

We advocate that citizens create ideals on topics of importance to them. Society needs to focus on ideals such as truth, justice and courage, to name a few. But as individuals, we need ideals about how citizens control their sense of agency. They must have control over themselves and their lives in order to accomplish the ideal sense of agency.

This clearly begins with the responsibility of the individual to know the truth. In an individualistic society, not only is speech protected, but the ability to make money, even by providing news, is acceptable. The challenge with this is, of course, that news stations, political parties, candidates and social media sites make money by getting you to watch them and endorse their views. And that has an effect on distorting the truth. But knowing the truth goes beyond this. It also includes you being truthful, most importantly to yourself.

And so our first ideal is to know the truth.

13

IDEAL 1: KNOW THE TRUTH

Understanding Agency

One's sense of agency is the awareness that one controls their own actions, behaviors or thoughts, and that through this control, they have an effect on outcomes. Owning one's sense of agency is also tied to the psychological "theory of mind." The origins of the theory of mind are not clear, but we know it dates at least as far back as the publication of *Meditations on First Philosophy* by René Descartes as a philosophical concept.[1]

In psychology, the theory of the mind refers to one's ability to discern another person's mental state and appreciate it as separate from one's own. It refers to the mechanism through which we can deduce what is happening in the other person's mind by discerning their intentions, desires, motives and beliefs that are different from our own. This is critical for everyday social interactions—in fact, a deficit in the theory of mind is considered a symptom of a neurodevelopmental disorder. Recent studies have uncovered neurological regions that are linked to the theory of mind through functional MRIs displaying activation, specifically in the right temporoparietal junction (rTPJ).[2] These experiments were designed to reveal processes linked to mental representation and reasoning of others' intentions, which is also considered a crucial component of moral judgment.

Much of the historical research regarding the theory of mind comes from psychological research into infant and child development by Andrew Melzoff, an American psychologist internationally recognized in this area. Melzoff recognized through his studies that infants understand others are like them, which allows them to also recognize others' physical characteristics and mental states while comparing them to themselves.[3]

The theory of mind develops in the child as the prefrontal cortex develops. The neocortex is the part of the brain responsible for sensation, perception, emotion and cognition. This cognitive part of the brain works very differently than the amygdala, which is responsible for the release of stress hormones that prepare our body for fight or flight.

The idea of an "amygdala hijack" was coined by Daniel Goleman in 1995 in a book called *Emotional Intelligence: Why It Can Matter More Than IQ*.[4] The term is descriptive of an earlier structure in the brain, the amygdala, which was designed to quickly respond to a threat. This threat may or may not be real, and it may come from something as simple as a conversation where voices rise and one person snaps. The individual loses their ability to respond rationally because the amygdala overrides the prefrontal cortex.

Returning to the theory of mind, this contains both cognitive and affective representations.[5] That is to say, it affects both our ability to understand others' mental states, beliefs and intentions (cognitive) and the emotions of others (affective). However, both of these can be disrupted by factors such as age, cognitive development and language development. The theory of the mind can also be affected by drug and alcohol consumption.

A study mentioned earlier in this book is worthy of mention again here. In "The Sociocognitive Processes of Ideological Obsession: Review and Policy Implications," in the journal *Philosophical Transactions of the Royal Society B*, researcher Jocelyn Bélanger describes four processes of an ideological obsession that puts one on a path towards violence.[6] These include:

1. Moral disengagement allowing unethical behaviors to happen without self-recrimination.
2. Hatred from ideologically obsessed individuals who are easily threatened by information that challenges their beliefs.
3. Gravitation towards people who think alike and possibly support violent thinking.
4. Shunning those they disagree with, making them immune to others who might persuade them to avoid violence.[7]

Our point in this study is that anyone can lose their sense of agency through ideological obsession, or what we call addictive ideologies. One's ability to understand, relate to and work with others can all be disrupted by ideology.

What's more concerning is that organizations who are motivated can take your agency from you—political party candidates, nightly news and social media have such motivations. By influencing you with fear-inducing information, they can instigate the amygdala hijack and release the stress hormones in you that stop you from using the part of the brain where optimism, rationality, creativity and empathy exist.

Paul and I, along with many of my colleagues, are seeing an increase in clients who are impaired and disturbed by the amygdala hijack that is all around them. The alarmist views are beginning to impact people who are becoming disillusioned, anxious, hopeless, panicked and paranoid. I surmise that what we are seeing in our clinics is a sample of the population that is fatigued from chaos, disharmony, instability and unpredictability.

Everyone has the responsibility to think about the agenda of the people behind the content they watch or read. What is the agenda of the nightly news? The moral agenda is to give you the facts of what is happening in the world. But because of the power of the negative bias, they are utilizing the amygdala hijack by telling you what is going wrong in the world. While it may not be a lie, it is out of perspective and a distortion of the truth, thus an inaccurate depiction. Their primary obligation is to shareholders, and this requires advertising. To get ads, they have to find a way to get you to watch tomorrow. And so, if it bleeds, it leads.

Social media is an even bigger offender in promoting conspiracy theories, false information, pessimism and negativity. At least in actual news outlets, while they may focus on the negative, they have some accountability to a self-imposed moral agenda to promote the truth—assuming you don't count the commentators who are on Fox, MSNBC and CNN as actual news. In our social media, we are not sure what the moral agenda is.

Social media companies such as Facebook and Twitter want the benefits of being both the free press and a capitalistic enterprise. They want the benefit of being media companies protected by free speech laws when it comes to opinions, yet they want the protections against liability laws that newspapers and nightly news must comply with regarding producing information that is not true. Companies like Facebook and Twitter are corporate behemoths that make money through selling ads, which target individuals based on the data these companies collect. That is promoted by the echo chamber we described earlier. They are incentivized to keep your eyeballs on their sites. Algorithms send you down rabbit holes of unregulated content—extremist opinions, disinformation, harmful and offensive rhetoric—ensuring that you will spend more time engaged with negative and potentially bad information. Incendiary content happens to be the category that gets the most comments, reactions and shares. Again, if it bleeds (or makes you enraged), it leads.

Research reveals that extended viewing of negatively biased news can impact the brain and psychological functioning. Normally, the brain selectively filters incoming information through the inferior frontal gyrus (IFG) and updates beliefs based on knowledge, experiences and new information.[8] Excessive exposure to negative news amplifies a cognitive bias that can impact our brains. It causes fatigue, anxiety, depression and negative moods.[9] According to Graham Davey, professor emeritus of psychology at the University of Sussex, "Doomscrolling bad news can make personal worries seem worse and cause acute stress reaction and some symptoms of post-traumatic stress disorder that can be quite long-lasting."[10]

Conversely, a bias towards optimism results in improved mental and physical health benefits, longevity and higher quality social relationships.[11] The *Oxford Handbook of Positive Psychology* (2021) revealed that people who have a positivity bias tend to cope with adversity by actively attempting to solve problems when they can, accepting problems that they cannot resolve and focusing on the positive aspects of their experiences. Regardless of one's dispositional tendencies, psychological research recommends limiting your time on negative news for improved mental health benefits,[12] and when exposed to negatively biased information, to counterbalance it with self-affirming and anxiety-reducing skills.

Political Parties Serve Their Funders—Not You

The goal of political parties is to serve the people who fund them. And after they elect someone in their primary, when only a small part of the public votes, they only then need to convince you that the other party is just a little bit worse. It becomes a very negative cycle that promotes division, distrust and pessimism.

America's political system has many problems, but it's still not as bad as each side projects against the other. So many people say, "our politics are broken." Actually, the system works just like the political parties want it to work. People often ask, "Is this the best the two parties can produce?" when in fact, the candidates we have to choose from are exactly the candidates the parties wanted.

The political parties are industries, as pointed out in the book *Political Industry:*

> Citizens accept as normal the system's decades-long retreat from deliberation and problem solving and its advance toward today's self-service and hyper-partisanship. We accept this new normal, in part because we are conditioned to help-lessness. We assume that our political system, warts and all, is a public institution governed by impartial laws dating back to the Constitution. But we would be wrong. Much of what makes up today's political system has no basis in the Constitution at all.[13]

The agenda of the parties is to promote the special interests that fund them. Not that special interests are inherently bad, but through closed primaries and gerrymandering, the extreme voices on both sides have a disproportionate influence compared to their actual numbers. Their agenda is to get you to believe that the other side's special interests are much worse than their special interests, and if given the opportunity, the other side will destroy the nation. So they darken the airwaves with negative ads about the coming of the apocalypse if the other party stays in power or gains power.

We support reforms that help give a greater voice to independent thinking. Based upon Paul's political career and experiences, he asserts that removing parties from exclusive control of the primary, subsidies given to the parties and gerrymandering are all areas worthy of change. We can choose to reject in-the-box thinking designed to divide us even further. From Paul's close firsthand experiences within the inner mechanisms of the political system, he can verify that the ideology of our current parties is to turn the "shining city on the hill" into an extremist state. Paul advocates that if you don't want their negative propaganda to register as an "Other" voter.

George Washington warned us about political parties. He was an independent and preferred a government and elections without parties. But if you were going to take part in a party, Jefferson's advice might be more beneficial. Jefferson said, in a letter to Thomas Hopkins:

> I never submitted the whole system of my opinions to the creed of any party of men whatever, in religion, in philosophy, in politics, or in anything else, where I was capable of thinking for myself. Such an addiction is the last degradation of a free and moral agent. If I could not go to heaven but with a party, I would not go there at all.[14]

The idea is you should not submit the entirety of your opinions to any organization where you are capable of thinking for yourself. You are an individual. It is fine to take part in organizations, but use rational thinking, reject hate or negativity, don't label others and don't put blind faith in the party—instead, find faith in yourself.

Politicians Get Elected by Terrifying You

Based on Paul's time in politics, he has learned that politicians come in two flavors: those who want to inspire you and those who want to terrify you. It is becoming more difficult to find the ones who want to inspire you. From Paul's firsthand experiences, he can confirm that politicians live in a certain time frame, and in a very short period of time, they need to convince you to vote for them over the opposition. The simplest and most effective way to break through the clutter is to incite your emotions, to make you believe you are being threatened and they are offering the solution.

The threat they present is designed to make you believe we are in a crisis. Because when people face a great crisis, they look for a leader who can protect them. It's not a new narrative that is most often told: The story is that the crisis is either being caused because of immigrants or the wealthy elite. Both become targets. Both have been used throughout modern history as scapegoats for radical revolutions. The challenge is when one side goes negative and the other responds, it can be difficult to see the difference between a tyrannical leader that will eventually deliver you to an authoritarian state and a democratic leader who will convince you that together, we can solve our problems.

Churchill and Hitler were both dynamic leaders in the 1940s. Understanding the difference between the two can become a powerful reminder of what we should expect from a good leader if we hope to continue to self-govern. One of those leaders represented the darkest side of human nature. Hitler was extremely successful in convincing his people that there was a common enemy, and that he alone had the power to save them. Churchill, on the other hand, inspired his people to believe that they held the power to build toward a better future. He told them that all he had to promise was "blood, toil, tears and sweat," but also that they came from a great history, a great people. And that together, they would be victorious.

The most important leader in a Western democracy is one who knows that through self-governance comes self-obligation. Self-obligation is tied back to that special thing within us, the power of the inner self. This leader is the one exalted by the Stoics, Martin Luther, Jefferson and our Constitution. This great leader we speak of is you. You have to lead when it comes to your own life. And to lead in your own life, you must demand inspiration, not demonization; love, not hate; the light, not the darkness. If we do this, our lives will not only be better, but our democracy will be safe for a long time to come.

It is something you should hold with great pride: Western liberal society places its focus on the individual. Our morality, our construct, believes that the individual is a wellspring of innovation, creativity and productivity that, when concentrated, benefits the collective. Thus, we base our beliefs on liberties and freedoms. We in Western democracy value freedom. But freedom is not a universal value. Some countries value the collective over individuals. Some value religion over individuals. And then there is the most universal value of all: power. Revolutions are fought over values. Freedom is simply not as valued as religion or the acquisition of power in most revolutions.

Fundamental to the idea that the individual should come first is the belief that there is a power within each of us. This power, it is believed through the most widespread distribution, results in the best society. We spread that power out through balance, as required by our Constitution. The executive, legislative and judicial branches of the government are equal branches. We may have a leader, but that leader still has checks and balances.

In the Federalist Papers (Feb 18, 1788), James Madison said:

If men were angels, no government would be necessary. If angels were to govern men, neither external nor internal controls on government would be necessary. In framing a government which is to be administered by men over men, the great difficulty lies in this: You must first enable the government to control the governed, and in the next place, oblige it to control itself.[15]

He believed we needed to control the government so as to protect the individual. This tells us how men like James Madison, who drafted the Constitution, were weary of government. Our first executive, George Washington, spoke about how he was weary of presidents and political parties. In Washington's farewell address (Sept 17, 1796), he said:

However [political parties] may now and then answer popular ends, they are likely in the course of time and things, to become potent engines, by which cunning, ambitious, and unprincipled men will be enabled to subvert the power of the people and to usurp for themselves the reins of government, destroying afterward the very engines which have lifted them to unjust dominion.

The founders believed in the individual, and the greatest threat to the individual was the government—and more importantly, a tyrant. Washington wanted us to put our faith in the Constitution, not a man nor a party. Madison told us how important it was to have checks and balances, to guard against the abuses of government and the men who run them.

Stop for a moment. Think about how powerful this thought is: that empowering individuals through self-governance and by holding truths, including the truth that the individual has rights granted to them by their Creator, that those rights make them more powerful than any king, emperor, *Führer* or president. The most powerful men in the country cannot stop you from speaking out in the public square. Through this society focused on individuals, we built one of the mightiest nations in the history of the planet. If that human spirit and the power within us is strong enough to lead nations, then it is certainly powerful enough to determine the outcome of our own lives. This is the power within us.

Discover Your Own Truth

The real power to make a change in our lives rarely comes from a political or tribal leader. The real power to make change is within us—from Nelson Mandela sitting in his jail cell dreaming of the world that could be to my parents being exiled after their family members were tormented, tortured, shamed, stripped of their wealth and brutally murdered. Coming out of despair, each dreamt of a new life full of hope and optimism for their families.

All of these people find a similar story. That even in the darkest of times, we are presented with choices, and those choices determine who we are, not the concrete or mortar that may imprison us.

As a psychologist, I have met with prisoners, people accused of terrorism, immigrants and people requesting clinical treatment. The human mind is complex, and people are diverse. There is no universal approach for everyone. But nonetheless, I have witnessed common themes that led people towards destruction and other commonalities where people have found salvation. Many factors drive this but one choice matters: whether we are making decisions from a scarcity mentality or an abundance mentality.

There are vulnerable populations that, through no fault of their own, have been neglected, undermined or disadvantaged by society. Within those populations, in dire circumstances, I have seen people who found incredible opportunities, and I have found people who have destroyed their lives and the lives of many people around them. By understanding the resilience and strength of those who found success, we can learn a great deal. They can help us be grateful for what we have. They can teach us how people can survive on minimal resources. We can also find amongst them a resilient, empowered human spirit that lights the way.

A scarcity mindset creates pessimism and an abundance mindset allows for optimism. It is a time of introspection and asking, "Who do I choose to be?" We have two factions, the right and left, that act as if there isn't room for the other. They see the world in terms of scarcity. The scarcity of the left believes we have to limit the income of the wealthy to improve the income of the poor. The scarcity of the right believes that we have to limit the influence of immigrants to protect the dominant culture.

Water resources, air quality, food production and other major problems can all be looked at from a scarcity mindset or an abundance mindset. In his book *Abundance*,[16] Peter Diamandis makes the case that we live in an era of abundance, yet so many people believe we live in an age of scarcity. He presents a compelling case that we are not going to fall short of resources for the planet and mankind, but that through technology, we will actually have an abundance of resources.

Within the scarcity mindset, everything is binary. Either you are pro-labor or pro-business—as if you could be pro-labor without being pro-business. Either you are pro-business or pro-education—as if you could be pro-business without being pro-education. And you are either pro-God or pro-human rights—as if God opposes human rights. These things are tied together. Economic development and social programs are connected.

We have to gain control of the messages we let into our minds. We have to understand the agenda of those who spread negative messages. Often it is financial. But just as often, it is driven by scarcity. We don't need to ignore challenges or threats, but to embrace this beauty inside of us, we have to include messages of hope, gratitude, abundance and most importantly, optimism. And this is a choice.

Find Space for Optimism

For Americans, there is nothing more empowering than knowing the truth. The truth is always powerful, but in many places throughout the world, the future is questionable. Regardless of what the soothsayers tell you, regardless of the politician warning how the other party has destroyed this country, we are very lucky to be right here at this point in time, in this particular place. Our future is vast and unlimited. But you can only know this truth if you look beyond the political parties, the media and the politicians. Instead, look at the facts.

This is the age of alarmists. If you look at the past few years of published books or headlines, you will see that there is a prominent alarmist on almost any topic you could imagine. There is alarmism about challenges to democracy, the rise of China, the threat of global war, woke culture, globalism, climate change, the economy and immigration. The public is being battered with dark and bleak messages by a media philosophy that purports, "If it bleeds, it leads."

Americans, as well as citizens of other Western democracies, are bombarded with negative messages that leave them concerned that their children won't inherit the same gifts we inherited. They believe that China will overcome Western democracy, that our debt will bankrupt us and that we will lose the world currency, substantially driving down the quality of life for every American. They believe that our military may not be able to defend us, or that technology is going to put them out of a job and turn our nation into something out of a dystopian novel.

Yet there is significant evidence that none of this is true. Yale historian Paul Kennedy described the US this way: "Nothing has ever existed like this disparity of power, nothing. . . .The US is the greatest superpower ever!" He makes the point that we are dramatically different from the superpowers who came before us.

From a demographic, geographic and institutional standpoint, the US is in a much better position than its counterparts. According to professor Mike Beckley,[17] demographically, the US workforce is the most educated in terms of years of schooling and one of the most productive among the major powers—and it is the only major workforce that will grow throughout this century. We will add millions of workers over the coming decades while, in large part because of its one-child policy, China will lose more than 200 million workers and gain 300 million senior citizens.[18] The demographics of the US have been greatly enhanced because of the millennial generation.

Geographically and institutionally, the US cannot be competed with either. If you were going to design a nation from a geographical standpoint that was a fortress, the US is a blueprint. Canada to our north, Mexico to our south and two major oceans east and west. China and Russia, by contrast, are surrounded by adversaries.

And while US debt may be a problem that threatens our ability to maintain our position as the world's largest reserve currency, the real question is: Who would we lose it to? The Chinese manipulate the yuan constantly to maintain exports. In August 2022, the US Department of Treasury designated China a currency manipulator.[19] In Peter Zeihan's 2022 book *The End of the World is Just the Beginning*, he points out that China has increased its money supply from 2008 by over 800 percent.[20] Who would put their reserves in a currency that the

Chinese government was going to intentionally depreciate to expand their exports?

Another alarm ringer is that technology is going to wipe out large portions of jobs. We are seeing instead a very real possibility that the US will face a shortage of workforce. The US Bureau of Labor Statistics predicts employment will grow by 8.4 million workers from 2018 to 2028. There is significant mounting evidence that we might not be able to find enough people to fill the jobs we are creating. I am convinced when the first farming combines were created, farmers were concerned that people would be displaced by the machinery, which would ultimately cause massive unemployment. They could not imagine an economic expansion with televisions, radios, automobiles and the job growth that they would create. It is a guess, but some great economists disagree that technology is going to cause massive unemployment. A new report by the United Nation's Economic Analysis and Policy Division (EAPD) reported that the loss of jobs from technology and innovation is overstated, and that in fact, history shows us that technology creates jobs as well as displacing others.[21]

The fear of the US losing its global positioning is just that: fear. The truth is that the US makes up less than five percent of the world population, yet according to Credit Suisse in "Total Wealth of Countries in 2021," we make up 31 percent of the world's wealth, 35 percent of world innovation and 40 percent of military spending.[22] In 2022, according to the Forbes 2000, the US had 590 of the top 2,000 companies. According to QS Top Global Universities, the US has 50 out of the world's top 100 universities. There is nothing like this superpower, and the only real threat we have of losing it will come from internal forces, not external ones. Even there, we think there is significant evidence that we are not nearly as divided as the media narrative projects.

This book is not designed to argue out these facts. The

point is that the current news media, social media and books on social trends make significant amounts of money by convincing you that the world is getting worse. It isn't profitable to argue for optimism, yet we believe it's critical if we truly want to preserve Western democracy. But make this a goal: Question the negative news you are watching or reading, and understand that they have a financial incentive to invoke a fear and anger response in you. Then, make space for optimistic information.

For more on how to know your own truth and a link to our Optimistic American *podcasts, please scan the QR code above.*

14

IDEAL 2: YOUR UNIQUENESS ENTITLES YOU TO THE RIGHT TO BEGIN ANEW

T he gentle giant watched as I approached him. He had a massive body, broad shoulders, a bald head and tattoos on his neck and face, all of which belied the kind, gentle nature of this man wearing an orange jumpsuit, living in a minimum security prison. To protect his identity, I'll call him Gentle Jim.

Jim was a model prisoner in every way. He took classes. He studied and read. He wrote prolifically. He was a mentor to other men in prison on how to survive long-term incarceration. He protected young men who were smaller or weaker and susceptible to abuse by others.

As I walked in, he greeted me with a warm handshake. He opened the door for me and allowed me to enter before him. As we walked, prisoners and guards greeted him warmly. His politeness was unparalleled by my experiences in the most refined circles, much less prison—and his prison record revealed that this was not an act.

He was 40 years old. Twenty-four years before, at age 16, he went to prison with back-to-back sentences for a horrific murder that, on its face, did not match the man I witnessed in front of me.

I read the report about the murder. It was clear that the 16-year-old Jim had lied about what happened, and the man in front of me had come to terms with what he had done. He was now willing to tell the truth, admit to his guilt and accept the consequences as a result.

At 16, Jim had a friend who was two decades older than him. Jim admired this man and looked to him for protection and life direction, but this man had abused Jim's trust. An argument broke out between them. Jim found the man's gun and pulled it on him. The man kept taunting and ridiculing Jim. All Jim remembers was wanting him to stop and then pulling the trigger.

Jim told me that there has not been a day since that moment that he did not regret his decision, which was an impassioned, heat-of-the-moment impulse. Jim revealed that his actions all those years ago still play out as vividly as if they happened yesterday, continuing to haunt him. That split-second decision forever altered the course of many lives.

There have been some seminal Supreme Court rulings in the past decade that continue to influence juvenile justice policy. On January 25th, 2016, the US Supreme Court ruled in *Montgomery v. Louisiana* that its 2012 *Miller v. Alabama* decision, which struck down mandatory life imprisonment terms without parole for juveniles, must be applied retroactively. States are not required to relitigate sentences in each case where juveniles received a mandatory sentence of life without parole, but they must permit juvenile homicide offenders to be considered for parole.[1] These rulings set in motion a review of Jim's case.

Specifically in the decisions of *Roper v. Simmons*, *Graham v. Connor* and *Miller v. Alabama*, the Supreme Court found that minors are constitutionally and developmentally different from adults in their level of culpability.[2] Moreover, the Supreme Court ruled that the severest punishment must be reserved for juvenile offenders whose crimes reflect permanent incorrigibility.

In an article in *Psychology, Public Policy, and Law*, Grisso and Kavanaugh (2016) examine the sentencing of juveniles from the developmental perspective, offering guidance to judges, attorneys and experts who provide developmental evidence in juvenile homicide cases.[3] Their findings supported that childhood experiences (i.e., trauma, abuse and violence exposure), immaturity, peer influence, brain maturation and other hallmarks of adolescence (i.e., impulsivity, sensation seeking and recklessness) are important factors for psychologists to consider in making evaluations.

My job was to evaluate Jim's psychosocial, emotional and cognitive development, including traumas, contextual and other developmental factors based on the Miller and Montgomery rulings.

This is an arduous task by all sides of the system, for the prosecution, defense and judge/trier of fact. My job was to provide a psychological evaluation in an objective, unbiased, scientific and methodological manner. The typical analysis of this type of case generally takes approximately 60 to 80 hours. Through that process, not only do we gain an understanding of the person, but the evaluation process, behavioral observations, testing results, collateral interviews, review of extensive records, validity measures and empirical research helps to support the findings and foundation for the expert opinion in response to the referral questions.

In conducting these evaluations, I have gained insights not only into people convicted of heinous crimes at a young age, but also what type of interventions may be helpful and when criminogenic factors, long-term incarceration and the effects of institutionalization may impact re-entry opportunities.

The job that I do matters, and seeking to understand the truth matters. The consequence of telling a lie or purposely omitting information is too big, regardless of the pressure. Understanding the human experience that underlies one's motive and mental state enriches the system by discerning the human being that it involves. The legal system will often attempt to distort the aggravating and/or mitigating factors to explain that either the person is "mad" versus "bad." The complexity of the human experience can show us it may very well be both.

One of the challenges of the American legal system is that it is designed around winning or losing rather than preserving restorative justice. Lawyers on both sides want to prevail and win, while it is the role of the trier of fact (i.e., judge or jury) to discern the truth. Regardless of who retains me, I always strive to humanize the person I am evaluating.

Eventually, after many hours spent by Jim's legal team in preparing his case for review, a new 2021 Supreme Court ruling on *Jones v. Mississippi* held that a separate and specific factual finding of "permanent incorrigibility" was not required to sentence a person who was under 18 at the time of their offense to life without parole, leaving it up to the individual states to make their own determinations of juvenile life sentences without parole.[4] This was devastating for Jim and his case for parole consideration.

The Evil of Ideology

In 1973, a manuscript by Aleksandr Solzhenitsyn, *The Gulag Archipelago*, forever changed the world's view of communism. Many credit the book with the downfall of the Soviet Union.

Solzhenitsyn wrote about his decade of experience in the Soviet Gulag, the infamous network of forced labor camps. After serving on the German front and criticizing Stalin in a private letter, he, along with tens of millions of others, were sentenced to the gulag.

Solzhenitsyn would estimate that the Soviet gulags killed as many as 60 million people—20 million during the forced collectivization of agriculture that resulted in severe famine, 20 million during World War II and 20 million in Soviet labor camps. He estimates that one out of every six Russians was sentenced to the gulag, and one-quarter of those were killed.[5] Those who survived faced brutal cold weather, starvation, little or no shelter and alienation from loved ones.

Solzhenitsyn wrote in the *Archipelago* that he took account of his own life and his own sins before recognizing the sins of the Empire. He spoke of the Kulaks, farmers who had been very industrious. An early supporter of communism, he was part of an effort to redistribute the wealth from these farmers— but taking their land wasn't enough. He spoke of one town where 10,000 families (over 60,000 people) were taken from their farms and homes and sent to the freezing tundra where they would all die horrible deaths from exposure.

Solzhenitsyn, as he explains in his 2,000-page manuscript, kept the story in his head during his stay. Now written, his book outlines the basis for good and evil. He says that good and evil do not originate from a government or a party but inside each one of us. He talks about the dangers of ideology—how each one of us who are not in touch with our potential for good or evil can buy into an ideology and use it to perform horrendous acts.

Communism, the idea that the government needed to control the means of production, meant people could not own property. But because not all people would voluntarily give up their property, force was used to take it from them. And if those people were allowed to rail against the injustice of this, they could persuade others that the ideology had flaws. To the believer in communism, these property owners were evil, and this was a justification to do horrible things to them—not only for the government, but also for individuals.

Solzhenitsyn advocated for the individual and posited that any ideology demanding that you justify the means of harming other people to accomplish an end was in itself an enabler of the evil within us. To combat this, he said it was required that we speak the truth when we know something is wrong.

But is hiding from our own evil because we are doing it for a greater cause really so foreign to us in America? Today we see the extreme right promoting white nationalism. And on the extreme left, we see the weaponization of identity politics and cancel culture. We see fringe movements based on the idea that the patriarchy is responsible for all of our problems in society and through this, that all men are part of the problem. This promotes the idea that the system is corrupt and perpetuates the power of the white man. Through those ideologies on the left and the right, participants see people unlike themselves as evil, thus releasing the evil inside of themselves to participate in the demonization that ideology demands of them.

A psychology pioneer, Dr. Philip Zimbardo (who wrote a review for the cover of this book), led what had been both a controversial and famous study known as the Stanford prison experiment.[6]Zimbardo wanted to investigate the question: What happens when you put good people in an evil place? Does humanity win over evil, or does evil triumph? Zimbardo's simulation of prison life conducted in 1971 at Stanford University revealed shocking results.

Zimbardo's study reveals that there are not necessarily good versus bad apples, but that people are vulnerable to conforming to the social role they are expected to play. Zimbardo later wrote:

Our planned two-week investigation into the psychology of prison life had to be ended after only six days because of what

the situation was doing to the college students who participated. In only a few days, our guards became sadistic and our
prisoners became depressed and showed signs of extreme
stress.[7]

He also reflected upon how he too fell into the role of the
superintendent or prison authority.

Zimbardo's aim was to show that any normal person can
become an agent of evil.[8] In addition, in his latest book with
John Boyd, *The Time Paradox*,[9] Zimbardo discusses the condition of priming effects influencing memory. Memories can
become reconstructed and thus are imprecise. Zimbardo
concludes that politicians, trial attorneys and others can
employ priming words to implant false memories. Zimbardo
was at a leading edge over 40 years ago in revealing how easily
people can lose their sense of agency, and that this loss of
agency could be extrapolated by news media, social media,
politicians or parties to prime their supporters and distort one's
perception and reality.

Extremists on both sides represent a small faction of Americans. There are, however, large factions of Democrats or
Republicans in this country who either idolize Trump or demonize him, even though this ideology has isolated them from
people they love or care about.

It is important to speak the truth, especially when you see
an ideology or the structure it controls committing violence
against other people. But we have seen and been a part of
allowing that conviction to make us unwilling to listen to those
on the other side—to not understand the injustice that they
may be feeling.

Most egregiously, we have witnessed, treated and been a
part of isolating ourselves from people we love for the ideologies of people we don't even know. The same people who, in a
crisis, we would most depend upon for our safety. We have

allowed alienation for people who, if we called, wouldn't even think of not returning our call.

And yet, in therapy and evaluations, every once in a while I meet someone who is inspirational. Someone who found the key to a meaningful life, even in unbelievably bad conditions. Regardless of your conditions, the beginning place to find healing isn't on the outside of you; it's on the inside. But it does require forgiveness, letting go of the past, letting go of hate and finding love.

Speak the Truth, Especially to Yourself

There is no wrong answer to this question, but you should be honest with yourself. What is your primary desire? Is it money, power or making a difference? The key to identifying this is to not mix up strategy with values. Values are defined as one's core tenets that inform our thoughts, actions and emotions.[10] These are the things we deeply believe in. Strategy involves the things we do to move our vision forward. The greater purpose is why we exist, what we view as meaningful pursuit in our lives and why we do them. This answers the "why" (core values) question versus the "how" (strategy).

Next, ask yourself: Are the things you identified really your core values? Or are they strategies or tactics to help you actuate your values? This is important because your values should remain constant. The strategies and tactics can always change, but they should help you accomplish the things you value.

To gain a better understanding of your core beliefs, psychologists often ask key and deliberate questions to assist the person in getting to a deeper level. These cognitive therapy techniques may include an evaluation of your assumptions and beliefs about yourself, your future, others and the world in a general sense. Once assumptions about yourself are elucidated, the key questions would then include: "If that were true, what would that say or mean about you?" We often interpret information through a cognitive lens, and what is driving that focus may stem from deeper-seated, unresolved issues. Often one's purpose is inextricably connected to these core beliefs.

Notice that some things may fit into values versus strategy boxes. To one person, the value is to be a good dad and the strategy is to carve out time from their agenda to do this. But if that same person said that what they wanted was to find love, we would see that as the true value, with "being a good dad" as a strategy to find that. This is often best accomplished by thinking things through from the "why."

Why do you want more money? To have more time. Why do you want more time? To be a better dad. Why do you want to be a better dad? Because you want to find love. Maybe being a better dad is a value all in itself. Or maybe you know you want to be a better dad, a better son, a better husband and a better brother. Why do you want these things? Once you find the real value, you will see that over time, the strategies and tactics can change, but you know why you are doing them.

Often I hear integrity listed as a core value. It's important to ask why that is a value. Do you value integrity because you want people to trust you? And why do you want them to trust you? Find the answer to that question, and you have figured out what you really value.

If your goal is to create a business, you should ask why. Why create a business? What is the value that is driving this? There are many reasons to start a business, and making money is one. But if making money is the only value to starting a business, we have found it to be problematic for the entrepreneur. A good value might be that you like helping people. This might lead you to go into a healthcare service as a strategy. But if that value of helping people gets lost along the way, the business will flounder. The value has to run from you all the way to the person answering the phone. It's hard to make that happen when you really haven't spent time thinking about what the real value is.

Even in business partnerships, there are core values that motivate actions. Partnerships provide unique opportunities to create efficiencies, increase market size or add unique skills. But trying to understand the values of the different partners is the place to begin. If the values of one is to retire and exit with cash and the other is to expand and grow, they obviously have something different in each of their values. But if partnerships begin with each listing their values and then understanding the strategies and tactics to accomplish those values, alignment is easier to achieve.

Put the Plan into the Universe

Deciding on values, strategies and tactics is not enough. The three together form a plan. For issues like finding love, you need buy-in from family, friends, children and mentors. In a business, that plan needs customers, investors, partners and employees. To make that happen, you have to put that plan out into the universe.

A lot has been written on this idea that if you put something out into the universe, things begin to happen. Some think it's metaphysics, some say it's karma, some call it God and some call it luck. Let's just go with common sense. To build anything, you need help, and you can't get help without others knowing about it.

This does not mean that people who end up in bad situations caused them. There are things beyond our control. But we all must have a plan and then share it in order to gather input. Sometimes that input is negative. People will tell you, "You can't get this done," or question why you would want to do it. Instead of seeing them as trying to upset your plan, think about the idea that maybe they care about you and they don't want you to be disappointed. And it's important to understand that without disappointment, you cannot find meaning.

Take the input, be realistic and make alterations to deal with the caution, but move forward, staying true to your values along the way. The input may have resulted in a very different plan or a plan that had to be implemented in phases. But it will cause you to move forward, take the risk and get closer to the reward of meeting your goals.

For more on honoring your uniqueness and starting over, and for a link to our Optimistic American *podcasts, please scan the QR code above.*

15

IDEAL 3: MEANING OVER HAPPINESS

"He who has any why to live for can bear almost any how."

-Friedrich Nietzsche

Focus on Meaning, Not Happiness

While most of us will have many joys in our life, everyone will face disappointment as well. We experience tragedies and loss. In those times, we are understandably not happy. However, even when we are unhappy, we can find meaning.

Sometimes "meaning" is affected by external circumstances out of our control. As mentioned, Aleksandr Isayevich Solzhenitsyn was a Russian who fought in World War II and was imprisoned by the Germans. When he was released, he was imprisoned by Joseph Stalin in the gulag for eight more years.[1] During these brutal periods of his life when he was starved, tortured, forced into labor and robbed of his life, he would take account of his own responsibilities. He was said to have reviewed every transgression in his life. In *The Gulag Archipelago,* he wrote:

> There is nothing that so assists the awakening of omniscience within us as insistent thoughts about one's own transgressions, errors, mistakes. After the difficult cycles of such pondering over many years, whenever I mentioned the heartlessness of our highest-ranking bureaucrats, the cruelty of our executioners, I remember myself in my Captain's shoulder boards and the forward march of my battery through East Prussia, enshrouded in fire, and I say: 'So were *we* any better?'[2]

Viktor Frankl, in his book *Man's Search for Meaning,* outlined how one could find meaning even in the worst of situations. Frankl was a psychologist in Vienna who, along with his family, was taken to concentration camps and eventually ended up in Auschwitz. His stories of survival are incredibly inspirational.

In Auschwitz, he noted that nine out of 10 prisoners were told to go to the left, one to the right. While they did not know it, the nine were to be killed; the one on the right was sent to endure horrible conditions in slave labor. Frankl was selected to go to the right. Every member of his family would perish in the Nazi concentration camps.

He noted that in these camps, there were stages that prisoners went through. And at some point, when the conditions had taken an incredible toll on those sent to slave labor, he found that one needed a "why" to get through the challenge. Those who succumbed to the horror, fear, dread and misery would soon die of hopelessness.

He observed that when we are no longer able to change a situation, we are forced to change ourselves. He believed in free will and said that everything can be taken from a man except his will. In order to survive, he must find meaning.

Frankl pointed out that there are three primary sources of meaning:

1. *Creation*. Pursuing a life task—knowledge, experiences and skills. We create in our writings, our poetry, our thoughts, our art, our job or business. We can find meaning in creation.
2. *Love*. One can find love in their family and their children, helping others actualize their full potential or elevating people around them. But one can also find love in a sunset or looking at the stars.
3. *Suffering*. Frankl believed that through suffering, one could find the greatest meaning. I ask my clients in situations where they suffer, "How do you want to look back on yourself and your actions? How do you want to feel and perceive yourself? How might suffering be valuable? How might it strengthen your character?" I encourage them to let these questions guide them. Growth from suffering can inspire beliefs, values and goals.

While Frankl usually did not talk about the meaning he found for himself when he faced the horror of recognizing his family had all perished, he did talk about how others could find it.

One of my favorite stories he told was of a man who came to him in despair because years before, his wife had died. Frankl asked him, "Would your wife have been as upset as you if she had died first?" The man said she would have been even more upset. Frankl then asked him if she would have been able to survive this pain that he was now feeling. The man said no. Finally, Frankl replied, "Maybe the meaning you have in this situation is that you survived because she could not. Maybe you survived to save her from her pain."

My parents found meaning while living under a brutal dictator who had murdered and tortured their parents. Their meaning was simply to try and survive and to create a new life where their children would not suffer the same challenges they did for being Jews in Iraq. Sometimes meaning comes in a prison cell while helping others. Meaning is usually not just one thing. It can be as an entrepreneur and a parent, a teacher and a coach, an engineer and deacon, or a psychologist, a mom and a belly dancer.

A meaningful life can take on many, many forms, but it always is based on service to others. Now, there are many ways one can serve others. We can serve others in our personal lives, in business, politics and in religious institutions. The key is that it has to be meaningful to you. Some find that in focusing on the customer, others by playing music. Some find it by working in their church, synagogue or local school. Some coach little league or work with animals. Others find meaning in being a parent or a grandparent. A meaningful life is up to you.

Find Meaning in Being a Survivor

Dr. Esad Boskailo, a Bosnian psychiatrist, pulled up to a group of heavily armed men with black face coverings that concealed their identity. He was on his way to the hospital. The men instructed him to turn around and go back. Dr. Boskailo told them that it was important that he go into the city when one of the men took off his mask. To Dr. Boskailo's astonishment, it was his neighbor. The neighbor begged Dr. Boskailo to go back because they were under orders to kill everyone in the city. It was the first time the doctor understood that his country was in a civil war.

From there, he would see the horrors a war can bring. He was captured and put into a concentration camp. People he knew, and who he once considered neighbors and friends, abused him and other men in the camp. He was slated for "cleansing." His best friend was murdered. His wife and children had to escape. He shed light on the unimaginable inhumanity of war, the dark side of human nature and his heartfelt journey to US citizenship. We have included a link to our podcast recording here with him regarding his book *Wounded I Am More Awake: Finding Meaning after Terror*.[3]

By any stretch of the imagination, a prisoner of war in a concentration camp has the right to call himself a victim. But Dr. Boskailo proudly declares that he is not a victim, he is a survivor. He found forgiveness for his captors. This is key is understanding that we do not always choose our circumstances. But we do choose how we define ourselves.

The Dark Passenger

We often don't see victimhood in ourselves. We see other people that we criticize for playing a victim role. We see the damage that it does to them, and we are annoyed that they use the crutch of being a victim to avoid the hard work it takes to reap the benefits of what life has to offer. We see this in others, but we often do not see the dark passenger that rides inside of us. We do not see that often, we unwittingly fall into the same category as those we criticize for being victims.

We know that victims are stuck. That through their own creation of a paradigm, they can't really grow because they believe that someone or something else is holding them back. They cannot see options, and so they live in a place that makes them miserable. They are unhappy, and in return, they make the world unhappy around them. They do not attract opportunity because of their negative energy—in fact, what they attract is more misery.

When we look around, it is easy to spot this today in so many others. We see one group who speaks the language of victims through their criticisms of "the elites," the fake news, minority groups, immigrants and liberals. Another group uses the language of being a victim through their criticism of "privileged white men," evil corporations and law enforcement. Both groups might tell you they are not being victims, but their language tells us something else.

It is important to note that experiencing trauma and victimization is not the same as having a victim mindset. You can gain this mindset without experiencing trauma. Also, many people, like Dr. Boskailo in the story above, can experience trauma and avoid the victim mindset.

The victim mindset has many negative consequences for society and for us as individuals. Professor Rahav Gabay at Tel Aviv University (TAU) School of Psychological Sciences says that the tendency for personal victimhood which becomes a central part of the individual's identity has an "external locus of control," meaning they believe their life is completely under the control of forces outside oneself. Based on clinical observations, they found interpersonal victimhood had four main dimensions:

1. Constant need for recognition of victimhood
2. Moral elitism
3. Lack of empathy
4. Frequent mention of past victimizations[4]

The victim mindset reduces levels of empathy for others and makes us less willing to accept our responsibility for harming others. Groups preoccupied with their own suffering can gain an "egoism of victimhood," giving them the inability to see things from another's perspective.

Professor Gabay also pointed out that research shows individuals involved in violence tend to see their victimization as exclusive, and as the mindset develops it actually changes the way events are perceived and remembered. Professor Gabay also identified the three main cognitive biases for the victim mindset. They are interpretation, attribution and memory bias. The combination of these biases distorts perception, which influences the individual's behaviors toward others and causes them to experience a higher intensity and duration of negative emotions.

Charles Sykes emphasizes in *A Nation of Victims: The Decay of the American Character* that groups and individuals are competing in "Victimhood Olympics" to prove their suffering is greater than one another, and thus more deserving of, and entitled to, happiness and fulfillment.[5] Regarding this, Gabay and her colleagues note: "When these feelings of entitlement are combined with a high individual-level tendency for interpersonal victimhood, social change struggles are more likely to take an aggressive, disparaging and condescending form." [6]

This is also called hate.

However, in story after story that we have witnessed, our traumas do not have to define us. We can actually grow from trauma. We can use our trauma to help other people and to make ourselves better. This is only possible if we lose the hate. If we start with love. We may need some tools to better understand how, but nevertheless, we can.

Understand Free Will

If you are not familiar with the Karpman Triangle (known also as the Drama Triangle[7]), it is a tool developed by Stephen Karpman to assist with unhealthy relationship dynamics. Dr. David Emerald authored a book based on Karpman's theory, *The Power of TED (The Empowerment Dynamic)*,[8] which is an easily relatable story. In it, he describes an unhealthy relationship that is driven by manipulation.

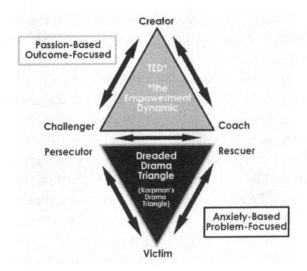

In the Drama Triangle,[9] each corner of the triangle represents a role—the victim, the persecutor and the rescuer. The victim sees himself as being bullied by the persecutor. The victim will often hook another soul into saving them. That poor soul is the rescuer. If the advice or contribution of the rescuer fails, often the victim will shift roles and become the persecutor, blaming the rescuer.

In this triangle, roles change quite often. Rescuers, through their advice, can often be seen as critics. Worse, if the rescuer actually fixes the problem, it makes the victim feel even more inadequate. The persecutor often sees themselves as the victim, causing them to complain about the victim for not living up to their needs. Both the savior and persecutor leave the victim feeling helpless and dejected, with no way to truly fix the problem.

These victim relationships often exist in alcohol and drug addiction environments. However, they can also exist with overzealous parents or inside companies. Increasingly, these victim relationships exist in our politics and our social structure. Part of addicting a person to an ideology is to turn them into a victim. Both political parties are in the game, one blaming the wealthy, the other blaming immigrants and both blaming the elites.

The key to this is to understand that we have free will. We choose to be the victim, the prosecutor or the rescuer. No psychologist, in our experience, ever expressed the issue of free will better than Viktor Frankl.

In 1942, Frankl was a prestigious doctor in Vienna. That year, he and his wife were forced by the Nazis to abort their child. Later, he and his family were arrested and deported to Theresienstadt Ghetto, north of Prague. Here, in a ghetto formed to torture Jews, his father died. In 1944, Frankl and the rest of his family were transported to Auschwitz. There he said, the Nazis would send nine people to the left and one to the right. He was separated from his family and sent to the work camp. The rest of his family died by the abuses of the Nazis.

Frankl spent his entire life teaching others about their power to choose. From his horrific experience, he understood that each of us, regardless of where we are and regardless of the conditions, have power over our own attitudes. He said:

> Everything can be taken from a man but one thing: the last of the human freedoms—to choose one's attitude in any given set of circumstances, to choose one's own way.

Sometimes making the choice to not be a victim is hard. It certainly was for Frankl. But our choice to not be a victim starts with seeing our choices, understanding how others are trying to manipulate us (specifically in politics and news) and choosing another way.

Become a Creator

Escaping the victim triangle is no easy task. Each of the participants—the victim, the persecutor and the savior—have to adjust their points of view. The alternative to the drama triangle is for the victim to see themselves as the creator, the persecutor as the challenger and the savior as the coach.

Any parent who has done too much for their children understands the problem of entitlement. Any employer who has created a hostile environment for employees who make mistakes knows the negative effect on innovation. Because each of these roles is interchangeable, we have all found ourselves in any of the three roles at any given time. To accomplish better results, we have to try and play a different role.

Even in prison, people can make the choice to educate themselves, to help other people, to exercise—or they can make the decision to be angry at society. But the first step for a victim is to truly identify the choices they have rather than be constrained by their limitations. One other example is for the victim to accept the faults of the persecutor. The persecutor also has limitations, needs and wants. The victim has many choices: accept the persecutor for who they are, move away from them, look for common ground, have conversations with them or simply recognize that limited communication between the two may be the only way.

The persecutor is most closely aligned with the victim. They too see themselves as being victims. To help themselves, they have to understand their choices. But to truly influence the other person, they have to move from being a critic to inspiring the victim to do better. That happens through positive reinforcement, having honest conversations and understanding how to find common ground. This is the persecutor's dilemma. They can either decide to be a victim themselves or recognize the responsibility that they hold in getting the future they want.

The persecutor and the victim usually are interchangeable roles. The persecutor feels victimized, as does the victim. The key for both is to see the other person for who they are, to understand their limitations, to not objectify them or label them and to see them as people who have faults like everyone else.

The person who sees themselves as a victim often can change the balance of power by attacking the persecutor. While the balance of power may shift, what does not change is being stuck in the drama triangle. The victim who now knows this becomes the persecutor, which only exacerbates the problem by making both people feel as if they have no choice. The result can leave people alienated, disconnected, angry and resentful.

For the savior, as long as they create an environment where they are bailing out the victim, it is inevitable that the situation turns on them. Any parent who tries to hang on to control for too long to "save" their child soon understands that the child does not benefit. The child either becomes more dependent or rebellious. Either way, the results are not what the parent wanted for their child or themselves. The savior has to begin to see their role instead as a coach.

Many of us grew up with religious stories. Regardless of your faith, you can find meaning in many of these stories. One of our favorites is the story of Cain and Abel. Cain saw himself as a victim. He saw Abel, who is depicted as the perfect one, as his persecutor. Cain could not live up to Abel's standard. Potentially, Cain's parents, Adam or Eve, tried to be the savior. They may have tried to save him by comparing him to Abel, which perpetuated Cain's victimhood. Had they played a role in helping him create his own pathway as his coaches, the outcome may have been dramatically different.

The sin was at Cain's door: the envy of his brother Abel. While true, simply identifying that envy is a problem or a sin may offer very little benefit. The approach to solve this problem requires a different strategy. A coach should instead start by asking Cain, "What do you want out of life? Are there other things that you might want to accomplish?" Oftentimes, by exploring what we really want, we find the standards and norms promoted by our imposed social construct are not the life we want.

How do you become a creator of your own destiny? In the victim triangle, if the victim can move from having limited options to unlimited options, they are empowered to create the life they dream about.

For more on free will and finding meaning, and for a link to our Optimistic American *podcasts, please scan the QR code above.*

16

IDEAL 4: LEVERAGE YOURSELF

There is a link between the partisan divide in our political system and what is happening on American college campuses today. In our American political system, we see growing friction to live and work with one another, propelled by our elected officials' increasing failure to cross the political aisle and improve the lives of the people they represent. On college campuses, speakers are shouted down and forums of discussion are canceled altogether. Professors know that talking about controversial ideas can not only get them canceled on social media, but it can also get them fired. Both students and professors know they cannot speak openly. And coincidently, rates of anxiety, depression and suicide are rising.

In the book *The Coddling of the American Mind,*[1] psychologist Jonathan Haidt and First Amendment expert Greg Lukianoff link the problems on college campuses to social norms that begin with childhood. The authors evaluate the beliefs "What doesn't kill you makes you weaker," "Always trust your feelings" and "Life is a battle between good people and evil people." They advance the theory that the adaptation of these false premises—and what they call the culture of "safetyism"—interferes with one's necessary social, emotional and intellectual development. It leaves young people with the inability to navigate the natural friction that comes through social interaction.

Lukianoff and Haidt define safetyism as a culture that treats safety of all types, including emotional safety, as an absolute right. This results in participants (students, teachers and professors) sacrificing emotional safety for other morally beneficial considerations such as fairness, free speech or even better mental health. They highlight beliefs emerging from this safetyism including the ideas that intentions don't matter, emotional pain or discomfort is dangerous and speech can be akin to violence.

The authors argue that these beliefs leave students to self-identify as emotionally fragile and in need of protection from words, ideas or individuals. They further argue that the adaptation of these beliefs and behaviors can hinder students' intellectual and emotional growth by making them more anxious and less resilient.

Lukianoff and Haidt's work, along with ensuing events on college campuses, have ignited research from other cognitive and experimental psychologists to further explore these social issues. In a recent follow-up study that analyzed the correlation of the "coddling" features, researchers assessed several variables that were found to be significantly associated with the rise of safetyism.[2] These authors looked at one of the controversial claims of the book, that safetyism-inspired beliefs, at least in part, are connected to cognitive distortions in college students. Cognitive distortions include catastrophizing, all-or-nothing thinking and the belief that one's feelings accurately represent reality through emotional reasoning. In their analysis, the study provided an empirical examination of the association between students' self-reported cognitive distortions and endorsement of safetyism-inspired beliefs. They found students self-reported that their "cognitive distortions" predicted their endorsement of safetyism-inspired beliefs that words can harm and support for the broad use of trigger warnings.[3]

Further research has indicated a strong psychological relationship between white identitarianism (alt-right) and political correctness authoritarianism. Mainstream personality traits associated with moderate political attitudes are well established; on the other hand, research into extreme political attitudes is just in its infancy. In a research article by Jordan Moss and Peter J. O'Connor, they examined the relationship between "dark triad" traits, entitlement and three extreme political attitudes: white identitarianism, political correctness authoritarianism and political correctness liberalism.[4]

The dark triad personality refers to three negative personality traits: narcissism, Machiavellianism and psychopathy (callousness and cynicism).[5] The word narcissism comes from the Greek myth of Narcissus, the hunter who became so obsessed with his reflection in the water that he eventually drowned. Narcissists can be arrogant, boastful and sensitive to criticism or insults. While they may act superior or entitled, it is often a cover for deeper-seated insecurities and inadequacies. Machiavellianism is named for the ruthless strategist in Italy who wrote *The Prince*. These individuals are manipulative, amoral, self-interested and deceitful. They have a negative view of the world and are willing to go to great lengths to ruthlessly deceive others for their own gain. And finally, the traits of psychopathy are defined as antisocial, volatile, remorseless and lacking empathy. They are usually cold, impulsive and prone to taking extraordinary risks.

This study found that these dark triad traits were not necessarily tied to political correctness liberalism, which is usually based on compassion, but was associated with white identitarianism (alt-right) and political correctness authoritarianism.

These two groups are deeply identified with similar traits that include a lack of compassion, empathy and a moral compass. They are willing to exploit anyone—including their closest family members—to get ahead, and experience little remorse when inflicting harm on others. They can engage in dangerous behavior regardless of how it affects anyone else.

The participants of both ideologies believe they are the answer to the abuses of the other. Many people consider white identitarianism as being at the opposite end of the political spectrum from political correctness authoritarianism, yet research shows that in terms of their dark profile, they are very similar.

The research of Dr. Jocelyn Bélanger with the Department of Psychology at New York University Abu Dhabi (mentioned previously in this book) supports these findings. Again, to summarize this research, Bélanger described four processes upon which ideological obsession can promote a pathway to violence. Those processes are first, the obsession over an ideology deactivates the moral self-regulatory process, allowing unethical behavior without self-recrimination. Second, as the ideology becomes more solidified as a mental construct, the individuals become easily threatened by any criticism, even factual information, which in turn leads to hatred and violent retaliation. Third, individuals obsessed over ideology repulse those who disagree with them and surround themselves with like-minded people who often further the ideological addiction and support violence—and as these social networks become more interconnected, they amplify one's adherence to violent extremism. Fourth, ideologically obsessed people are prone to psychological reactance, making them immune to communication strategies designed to make them less violent.

Where psychology meets philosophy is when we look at these psychological issues in relation to the philosophers whose ideas were the foundations of our democracy. The concept of free speech as espoused by John Stuart Mill in *On Liberty* discusses the eternal "struggle between authority and liberty." Mill saw the tyranny of the majority as a greater evil than the tyranny of government because it was harder to control, and he felt we should be equally concerned with the "tyranny of the prevailing opinion and feeling."

To Mill, the fear of prevailing opinion and feeling was not about natural rights, it was about the usefulness of the opposing view. Just because an opinion is the view of the majority does not make it right. Mill believed one could hold three types of beliefs: wholly false, partly true and wholly true. All benefited the public good. He pointed out that even though a statement may be untrue, it may hold some portion of the truth. And the only way to understand what part was true was through robust discussion.

Part of Mills's point was that discussion was key to the survival of democracy and the authority of the individual. Without such right to speech, where discussion could lead to better outcomes, democracy would eventually fail, because quite often, the original prevailing opinion was wrong.

With political correctness and cancel culture, we may actually be facing the tyranny of the minority. Prevailing thought can be determined not by a majority, but by a system of bullying where others stay silent, believing they are a minority.

Reputation denigration is a powerful tool of cancel culture. The overwhelming majority of people hope to tie into existing society—to get a job, start a family, own a company. All these necessary functions relate to one's ability to maintain a decent reputation. Labels such as racist, homophobic and bigot, along with many others, can have powerful impacts on one's reputation, and thus their ability to participate in society.

The dark triad within white identitarianism uses violence as a way to stop opposition.[6] Within political correctness authoritarianism, the use of insidious labels through social media can destroy one's reputation. The narcissist, Machiavellian or psychopath has no problem utilizing such devices to destroy others, regardless of the truth and regardless if it diminishes the value of such terms—so long as it raises the social stock of the accuser.

Christopher Carpenter, an assistant professor of communication at Western Illinois University, studies the dark side of Facebook. Carpenter's study, "Narcissism on Facebook: Self-promotional and anti-social behavior," published in the journal *Personality and Individual Differences*, asserts that for the average narcissist, Facebook "offers a gateway for hundreds of shallow relationships and emotionally detached communication." More importantly, this study purports that social networking in general "allows the user a great deal of control over how he or she is presented to and perceived by peers and other users."

According to Carpenter's study, individuals with the dark triad traits, specifically narcissists, have more friends. Their controversial content has higher engagement. As the studies above mention, ideologies have the ability to take more extreme measures when their ideological construct is challenged. In this way, the dark triad may be less about genetics than about a physiological feedback loop.

Psychopaths make up less than one percent of the population.[7] They have a criminal mindset, egocentricity and lack empathy and remorse. Research reveals that there is a lack of compelling evidentiary support for treatment approaches for psychopathy.[8] Fortunately, there are only a few in society—but world history has shown it does not take many to disrupt society. As psychopaths attract others to their cause, atrocities expand. On social media, little or no regulations or punishments exist in creating an incentive for bad behavior.

With the alt-right, the dark triad personalities drive it towards violence. With the politically correct authoritarians, the dark triad turns towards destroying reputations. Reputation is important to the success of almost any individual. But on university and college campuses, among professors and administrators, reputation is everything. They are particularly vulnerable to challenges of their reputation based on bigotry. And while part of the stress from cancel culture and political correctness on campuses may come from generational change, administrators play a role as well by not bowing their back.

Universities are generally successful at protecting against the dark triad mindset that might incite physical violence through zero-tolerance policies. However, dark triad mindsets that promote damage to reputations can often be unwittingly enabled by college administrators who are often concerned about their own reputation. As an example, if a college professor is accused of bigotry, the accusation can be so incendiary that it ignites strong passions amongst a prevailing opinion of the student body. The administrator concerned about damage to their own reputation may take action against a professor or not provide them with adequate support. This can be without due process, and it may be without due diligence or understanding of the facts that underlie the professor's comments. In such an environment, it becomes easier for some people to take advantage and manipulate others for their own self-aggrandizement.

An atmosphere of accusations and fear can unfairly damage reputations, but it can also damage the culture of learning, intellectual stimulation and growth through debate and challenge. Safety is important, but alongside protecting student safety, we need to help them build resilience. That means we have to give equal value to strength, truth, fairness and sometimes forgiveness. Intentions have to matter.

For most of us, we stand between these two groups of politically correct authoritarians and the alt-right. Neither of these groups are looking for equality but instead for their cause to dominate over the other. They scream and yell at one another and are unwilling to listen to the other side. And this majority who stand in the middle, who just want the rage, hostility and uncertainty to end, cannot allow the rules to be set by the narcissist, the Machiavellian or the psychopath. We must stand firm by the values that our land was founded upon: fairness, due process, truth and free speech. It will create friction, but through that friction, we will build resilience.

For more on leveraging yourself and avoiding safetyism, and for a link to our Optimistic American *podcasts, please scan the QR code above.*

17

IDEAL 5: FIND POWER IN LOVE AND CONNECTION

"You should respond with kindness toward evil done to you, and you will destroy in an evil person that pleasure which he derives from evil."

-Leo Tolstoy

In the book *Younger Next Year,* author Chris Crowley, a cellular biologist, gives advice on how to stay younger. His first two pieces of advice are expected: diet and exercise. But what stands out in his book is his description of the need for humans to be connected to others. He details what happens at a biological level to humans, and all mammals, when they are disconnected.

One of the stories is about a herd of deer. In this herd, there is always a group of does who surround one buck. Other bucks live for years on the outside of the herd alone, but one day, one of those young bucks will come into the circle and challenge the big buck and win. The big buck then must go to the outside of the herd. They never live for more than a few months.

The author points out that it is not a statistical anomaly that for couples who have been married more than 50 years, when one dies, the other often dies months later. Loneliness does not just hurt, and it is not only bad for your health. It is a killer.

Human beings have an innate desire to be connected. Whether we know it or not, we crave love. Multi-billion-dollar corporations have built models on this very issue, giving us the ability to friend people and show support for them by "liking" their posts.

At the beginning of this experience, we shared pictures of our families, great adventures and milestones as a way to let our friends and family know about our lives. Today, most of these social networks have become a graveyard for friendship and a Petri dish for addictive ideologies, political positioning and corporate sales. You cannot achieve true connection by simply finding people online who hate the same people you hate. But you can find a way to create resentment, discord, anger and maybe even stoke violence through hatred.

This hate is not limited to digital platforms or specific political parties. Hate is perhaps the most universal and bipartisan issue most of us can agree upon. In Congress, Democrats and Republicans express their views toward one another with disdain, distrust and dishonor. The once-united fights for equality have been replaced by proclamations of superiority on both sides.

Yet, we know from polling that this does not represent a majority of Americans. Most of us want to lean into that other unifying issue: love.

Change How We See and Address Others

Dr. Martin Luther King, Jr. was more than just a great civil rights leader. He was a great spiritual leader for everyone. There were many reasons that would have justified Dr. King to be driven by anger, resentment and hate. The conditions under which most Black Americans lived during the Jim Crow era were deplorable and shameful to this nation. Though slavery was outlawed, many lived as prisoners to segregation, violent racism and laws designed to oppress any chance of opportunity and equality that the Emancipation Proclamation (signed in 1863) promised. Speaking out about this unjust reality could be a death sentence.

But Dr. King spoke about love—and not the wishy-washy "let's all be friends" pacifist love he is often misidentified as preaching. Dr. King's idea of love was revolutionary. He pointed back to the definition of love from the Stoics who believed there was a difference between romantic love (*eros*), platonic love (*philia*) and a love known in Greece as *agape*. Dr. King defined this not as a sentimental emotion but instead said:

> We speak of a love which is expressed in the Greek word agape. Agape means nothing sentimental or basically affectionate; it means understanding, redeeming goodwill for all men, an overflowing love which seeks nothing in return.

He was looking to build a sustainable new world. He wanted equality for his people, but he wanted to get it by being close to his oppressor, trying to understand him and, maybe more importantly, forgiving him.

He asked: "Why should we love our enemies? The first reason is fairly obvious. Returning hate for hate multiplies hate, adding deeper darkness to a night already devoid of stars. Darkness cannot drive out darkness; only light can do that.

Hate cannot drive out hate; only love can do that. Hate multiplies hate, violence multiplies violence and toughness multiplies toughness in a descending spiral of destruction."

Before we can be successful with any movement, we must start with the basic moral intent of seeing others with dignity. That is the only way for them to see us with dignity in return.

The Labels We Give Others Reveal Our True Selves

Becoming a victim is not limited to people who have suffered from a catastrophic event or who have committed crimes and are in prison. I have found a strong connection between people who see themselves as victims and people who label others. The language they use is a giveaway to seeing who has a victim mindset. The victim will see themselves without options and believes there is almost always someone else to blame. In a marriage, this mindset can be revealed by the names they apply to their spouse. In politics, they might generalize the persecutor or the oppressor, usually blaming the rich, corporate America or immigrants. The victim mindset goes hand in hand with labeling and objectifying the public oppressor.

The reason we create labels for people is to objectify them. If you can label someone as a feminazi, it becomes easier to ignore the points that the person is trying to make about gender equality. If you see a conservative as a fascist, it's easier to ignore the input on the importance of maintaining a budget. Objectifying another person creates in our own mind a justification for our own inequity, irrationality or failure. It is a betrayal of ourselves and it limits our ability to grow. It prevents us from understanding others and understanding ourselves.

When we label people, we have begun the process of dehumanizing them. Labeling becomes a justification for the wrongs we commit. In addition, we begin to create a false reality. By putting other people into a box, we also begin to put ourselves into one. Calling someone a bitch, a Nazi, a liberal, a conservative or any other term that might be used to label someone else gives us the ability to no longer see them as individuals, but instead, as objects. And once we see them as objects instead of as humans, our ability to aggrieve them unfairly becomes justified.

In the story of Omar, it was clear that he had a series of labels for those people whom he had harmed. This included not only demonizing American values but oftentimes demonizing people of a different religion than him by labeling them infidels. He also demonized people of his own faith who had differences in dogma by calling them heretics. When being indoctrinated into an extreme sect, one of the goals is to institutionalize the idea of a victim, then apply black-and-white standards to people that fall within the labels. Another goal is to remove the individual from victimhood by giving them opportunities to vindicate the cause.

Here, the victim triangle is not self-imposed but instead weaponized by political or religious leaders attempting to create a faithful following. The only protection one has from a political, religious or cultish leader would be to recognize the leader's use of labels as a means to divide people. That can be very difficult for those who find themselves oppressed or believe they have no options.

Hate and Envy Hold You in the Past; Love Sets You Free

The story of Gentle Jim is that of a man who, in the direst of circumstances, created meaning for his life. Happiness can be fleeting. All of us can find our periods of happiness disrupted by events that make us sad. But even in those moments of sadness, we can maintain our sense of meaning. Jim found true meaning because he believed in himself and the power within.

But Jim would not have been successful had he begun with

hate. He could have easily felt hate for the lover who abused him, hate for the society that discriminated against him, hate for the life sentence in prison imposed on him for something he had done as a boy. But hate would have held him in the past, and he would have been unable to move forward. He could only be successful by beginning anew and doing so with love. Love and service helped him let go of his past and gave him a future.

Find Gratitude

Gratitude is more powerful than you can imagine. But sometimes it's hard to put into practice. It was hard for my parents, who lost their parents to a dictator. It was hard for Gentle Jim in prison. It was hard for Nelson Mandela, and for the founding fathers of our country when the war seemed lost. And it will be hard for you at times also.

Research has shown that those who deliberately practice gratitude can train their minds to see the world differently, reaping many benefits in the process. Studies have demonstrated that moral judgment involving gratitude is in the right anterior temporal cortex and that people who regularly express gratitude actually have higher volumes of gray matter in the right inferior temporal gyrus.[1] The effects, when practiced, can be as powerful as medication. Gratitude, when expressed, releases dopamine and serotonin, the key neurotransmitters responsible for our emotions and making us feel good.[2]

Joshua Brown, a professor of psychological and brain sciences at Indiana University, along with Joel Wong, an associate professor in psychology at Harvard University, both did separate[3] studies[4] on the benefits of gratitude.

Professor Brown and Professor Wong created three study groups of people who were already seeking mental health treatment. For three weeks, the participants of one group wrote a weekly letter of gratitude to another person. Another group wrote about their deep feelings regarding negative things. The third group did not do any writing.

The participants of the first group were found to have "significantly better mental health."[5] These participants would agree: gratitude frees people from toxic emotions, and it has long-lasting effects on the brain. All three groups underwent brain scans during the study, and those who practiced gratitude showed activity that indicated boosts in serotonin and dopamine.

Harvard Medical School reported, "In positive psychology research, gratitude is strongly and consistently associated with greater happiness. Gratitude helps people feel more positive emotions, relish good experiences, improve their health, deal with adversity and build strong relationships."[6] Harvard researchers recommended several ways to cultivate gratitude. Among them were prayer, meditation and the deliberate counting of one's blessings. Or as Abraham Lincoln famously said: "When you reach the end of your rope, tie a knot and hang on."

Be grateful for what you have. For the supporters of Western democratic values that place the individual at the center, we need to create strong individuals, not violent ones. We need to practice our ability to communicate, and we need to become resilient by listening. We must find love, compassion and connection, as well as practice gratitude for all that we have.

None of this is an abdication of our values. We all have the right to express our beliefs. But only through listening and understanding can we overcome the great challenges posed by a society based on the individual. This demands growth, courage, wisdom and love.

For more on the power of love and connection, and for a link to our Optimistic American *podcasts, please scan the QR code above.*

18

IDEAL 6: WE, NOT ME

"If there are people south of you, then there must be people north of you. There is no one north and no one south, just east and west at different levels on the horizon."

-Paul Johnson, Sr. (wise words from the author's father)

There is no greater gift than the one you get from giving. This is not just a mantra. It is a scientific fact that people who help others are healthier, less stressed and live happier lives.

Leadership is about giving, yet this is not the definition given by most people. What makes a leader, how people become leaders and those leaders who have the greatest impact are greatly misunderstood in society. Each of us, in our way, is called upon to be a leader—as parents, siblings, colleagues or members of our community. Leadership is not a skill that one is born with but a skill that one learns.

The first lesson of leadership is to understand that it is a responsibility, not a gift. A real leader sees their responsibility to help others, not opportunities for self-gratification. Throughout history, a leader has been associated with the power and acquisition of goods, from food to weapons. But imagine the leader in a tribe or village 100,000 years ago, using fear tactics and brute strength, terrifying other villagers and taking advantage of them. It is safe to assume that when the physical strength of this leader failed, they met an ignoble fate. In this imaginary village, the leader who prevailed would not necessarily be the best hunter of the tribe but the one who shared his kill generously with the others. This was the type of leader who could not only last a lifetime but often lived on in mythology as well.

Throughout history, there have been leaders who are self-serving. But overwhelmingly, those who found success as presidents, governors, mayors, CEOs, business leaders or heads of institutions gave much more than they took. There certainly are abusers of power, but they are the minority. Leaders who abuse don't last because sooner or later, they run out of people who are willing to follow them.

More importantly, good leaders understand the concept of "we, not me." The idea of self-made people who say they did it on their own is a myth. We all have teachers, family members and mentors. We all stand on the shoulders of giants. The signers of the Declaration of Independence put their lives on the line to "mutually pledge to each other [their] lives, [their] fortunes, and [their] sacred honor" for the rights that eventually led them to own what they would create and to benefit accordingly. Real leaders respect this and are grateful for these gifts.

You Live in the Greatest Time in History, in the Greatest Superpower Ever

By every measurable standard, the human condition is improving. There are many challenges that we still face as a species (from climate change to world hunger) and as a nation (from income inequality to racially motivated violence). But still, there is no better time or place to be alive than right here and right now. Steven Pinker is a Harvard professor and the author of *Enlightenment Now: The Case for Reason, Science, Humanism, and Progress.* This cognitive scientist and great public intellectual urges society to step back from the drama-filled headlines that play to the negative bias and instead follow the data. In over 70 stunning graphs, Pinker shows that life, health, prosperity, safety, peace, knowledge and happiness are on the rise, not just in the West, but worldwide.

On his website stevenpinker.com, he also lays out a warning:

> The enlightenment we know has worked. But more than ever, it needs a vigorous defense. The enlightenment project swims against the currents of human nature—tribalism, authoritarianism, demonization and magical thinking—which demagogues are all too willing to exploit. Many commentators, committed to political, religious or romantic ideologies, fight a rearguard action against it. The result is a corrosive fatalism and a willingness to wreck the precious institutions of liberal democracy and global cooperation.

This extraordinary progress did not happen by accident. It happened because more than 200 years ago, our founders decided to create a government where the individual was at the center—not a party, not a monarchy, not a government. The people, each as individuals, were at the center. From that, we created something that was almost unimaginable 100 years ago. And what we will create tomorrow and 25 years from now is unimaginable today.

In 1945, when most of the world was destroyed by war (with the exception of the United States), the US offered the world a grand bargain, partly through the Bretton Woods Agreement.[1] The deal was that we would spend money rebuilding other nations, and we would give them access to our financial markets. We had the only navy big enough to protect the safe passage of products on the oceans, and so we helped guarantee other nations' ability to buy and sell goods and allowed them to sell into the only market that had the ability to buy: the US market. There was one catch: you had to pick a side in the Cold War against the Soviet Union.

In 1972, Richard Nixon offered the same basic deal to China. The result of this was not only the greatest expansion of the world market in human history but the unprecedented human progress on poverty, literacy and other issues outlined by Pinker. In the concept of entropy, the world's natural state is disorder and poverty. Without these safeguards provided by the US, these benefits will fall at risk.

The US has benefited from this agreement as well. The US arguably could have become an empire in 1945, but that doesn't sit well with democracies. Instead, by helping other nations out, we built up an unbelievable alliance. Today, no other nation can boast our alliances: over 68 alliances with 587 military bases scattered over 42 countries. The US today, with less than five percent of the world's population, makes up 31 percent of the world's wealth,[2] 35 percent of the world's innovation and is home to 590 of the world's top 2,000 corporations. These things are connected. Our wealth partly came from the world order we created that in turn had a massive impact on world poverty.

We should be proud of who we are. This does not mean we

don't acknowledge mistakes nor how we can improve. But we have done more to move forward the human condition than anyone at any time. And if we preserve the individual being at the center and the power of free markets, we will fix the challenges of this generation as well.

We Empowered Individuals, but No One Came Alone

"Live as though God exists."

-Blaise Pascal

One of the many gifts of living in the United States is that individual effort is rewarded. That can leave many people believing that everything they accomplished they did alone, but if you take the most brilliant creators and put them in a different time and place, it is highly doubtful they would have had the same impact. The rule of law, as well as the rights of property and patent protection, are written into our Constitution, guaranteeing we can own and profit from what we create.

Professor James A. Robinson, in his co-authored book *Why Nations Fail*, argues that the failure of a state comes from extractive policies. A society can be extractive by the government or monopolies taking resources from the private sector. This inhibits the ability to innovate new ideas. It was through the rule of law and the property rights written into the Constitution that extractive policies were put in check, allowing people who work hard to come from the bottom of society to create, innovate and prosper while at the same time moving humankind forward. The great things that we may do or have done are partly because of those who came before.

We live under a social contract of our Constitution. That

document grants people the right to own what they create and to profit from their own labor, and it stops the government from being able to seize an individual's property for the public good unless they are compensated—and even then, there are extreme limitations. The Constitution was put in place and kept in place by the actions of men and women who gave everything they had for it—often including their own lives and the lives of their families.

We empowered the individual in our Constitution with the Bill of Rights, which included the right to free speech, assembly, religion and protected property ownership. We placed those rights above the rights of the government. We have prospered because our courts limited the power of government, forcing it to observe those rights. By holding the genius of the individual above all else, we enriched the collective, but we never put the collective over the individual. And yet you will find many individuals who put the collective over their own interest. These are the people we consider heroes. You find them in the firehouse, police stations and our schools. You find them on our military bases, on aircraft carriers, submarines, fighter jets, in intelligence and forward positions. You can find them in ordinary people who struggle to pay their bills, keep their kids in school and work hard. And you find them in the entrepreneurs who test the standards, who challenge the status quo, who push the thinking—to cure cancer, extend human life and create cars that drive themselves.

In America, you can also find these men and women in cemeteries across the country, those revolutionaries who risked their fortunes and lives in battles like Charlestown, Saratoga or Bunker Hill, or the 50,000 who died at Gettysburg in the war to end slavery. Those who died in the jungles of Vietnam, the deserts of Afghanistan, the island caves of the South Pacific, the freezing cold in the forests of Europe and the beaches of

Normandy. They came from beach towns in California, the plains in Texas, the high rises of New York and every small town and big city from coast to coast. They did not sacrifice as red or blue voters; they sacrificed as Americans.

Mankind owes a debt to those who sacrificed to protect the rights of the individual above all else. People like Washington, Jefferson and Lincoln. People like Harriet Tubman and Martin Luther King. These are among the many people who helped you along the way.

We know our rights, but we also have obligations according to that social contract. We have to live by the rule of law, free elections and the peaceful transfer of power. These issues are coming under question today, maybe because in our zealous desire to get what we want politically, we forget the many other benefits we obtain by holding this together, or maybe because power is a more universal value than freedom. But we should all live as though God exists. We should live understanding that we belong to something bigger.

It is not just the rich who have this entitled view of not recognizing their success came on the shoulders of people who sacrificed so they could prosper. You can see the same thing from people who denigrate our past, placing themselves as moral vanguards of values that they did not create.

It is important to understand that standing on the shoulders of giants benefits you. It makes you part of something bigger, something that you and those who come behind you can be proud of. We have our warts, but the arch of our destiny will do more to empower people with more rights than any other group before us.

Hold Our Heroes Dear

If you have to practice identity politics, then how about identifying with those who came before us, those who gave us the great gifts we have today? Although imperfect, this history made us who we are, and who we are is unique. We hold greatness in our hands. But it is a greatness we inherited, not one we invented alone.

In the United States, the ideals of Western democracy and the focus on the individual are only as strong as the people who believe in them. We face an internal threat today, posed as a question: "Is what we created worthy?" As stated earlier, identity politics is a problem when people identify with ethnic backgrounds that promote aggression. But if we stop identifying with what is good about America, then the values America represents become threatened.

Certainly, one of the scars on the face of America is slavery. Slavery is and was morally wrong. But some are condemning all of Western culture, the United States and capitalism, arguing it is corrupt because it was built on slavery and is thus morally corrupt from its foundation.

Maybe the right place to start is by asking why is slavery wrong. We can see two solid reasons. One: It is unethical for one group of people in power to be able to completely abuse another group of people because they don't have power. The abuses of American slavery were horrendous, involving breaking apart families, torture, murder, rape and castration. The second reason is even more powerful. It is the argument that comes from *thumos*, Martin Luther and others. Slavery is wrong because, in our society, the individual is central.

This concept of the rights of the individual being central is not universal. A substantial part of the world puts the rights of the collective first—as interpreted by a minority group, oligarchs or a king. The rights of the individual being central is an American-sprung idea from 1776, and while the US was first, this thought now dominates Western democratic thinking.

We believe that you cannot take away individual rights,

because doing so would deprive us of the gifts given to us by individuals. An attack on the individual is an attack on the central value we hold, that inside each one of us is something special, and that each one of us is worthy of dignity and equality.

This concept of individualism is a Western value. The alternative to this is the theory of the collective, whose rights are protected by a special class of people. In this model, all that matters is power. In this model, it is the party, the oligarchs or the tyrant that matter.

The question we should ask of our political leaders is not whether or not they are flawed people. The standard they should be held to is:

> We hold these truths to be self-evident, that all men are created equal, that they are endowed upon by their creator with certain inalienable rights. And among those are life, liberty, and the pursuit of happiness.

The role of government is to protect these rights; we should only ask, "Did they move this concept forward for mankind, or did they move it backward?"

Dr. Martin Luther King, Jr. was a man with many flaws. Certainly, his issues with women would struggle in the days of the Me Too movement. Yet he moved these "truths" forward, that all men are created equal. That they should be judged by the content of their character, not by the color of their skin. In this same light, our founders, some of whom owned slaves, should also be gauged by this standard.

While slavery is morally wrong, that immorality was not as universally accepted in 1776. However, those truths revolving around the individual were moved forward by men like Thomas Jefferson. The men who wrote those words risked all they had to overcome the King of England, who saw his job as protecting the collective. Jefferson, arguably more than any other, moved the power of the individual forward. While not the objective at the time, this concept would result in the idea that slavery is not only wrong but immoral.

If individualism is to survive, it badly needs heroes. In our past, both Dr. King and Thomas Jefferson were individualism's heroes, as were Abraham Lincoln and Fredrick Douglass. This does not mean we have to overlook their shortfalls, their sins or their flaws. But everything should be viewed within the perspective of how they moved individual rights and human dignity forward.

We deeply question those who attack our founders today. In doing so, these detractors claim authority for themselves through self-righteousness and provoking guilt. They risk harming the very thing they should want to protect: the individual being at the center. It was our founders' focus on the individual that inevitably led to the moral evolution that declared slavery was immoral.

We wonder about the actual goal of those who undermine our heroes. Is it self-aggrandizement? Or is it simply frustration that other historical heroes are overlooked? Certainly, we have room to add to the existing list of those who contributed to Western democracy, including women, people of color, LGBTQ people and members of other marginalized groups. But we don't have to destroy other heroes to do so. Again, we revisit the story of Cain and Abel (from Genesis 4:6-7 ESV):

> The Lord said to Cain, "Why are you angry, and why has your face fallen? If you do well, will you not be accepted? And if you do not do well, sin is crouching at the door. Its desire is for you, but you must rule over it."

Both brothers were men of means, Cain a farmer and Abel a shepherd. But God gave preference to Abel's sacrifices. God told Cain that envy would pursue him, but it was up to Cain to control it. When he did not, it resulted in him slaying his brother, and that was a sin too great to bear.

The risk of destroying the heroes of America is that we destroy the glue that holds our society together, and perhaps this may be the goal of some. But if you destroy that glue, you destroy the voluntary participation that is necessary for a society to work.

In the book *Sapiens* by Yuval Noah Harari, the author makes the case that mankind's greatest invention was myth. Through the creation of religion, cities, nations, currencies and even corporations, we created the ability to organize people into larger groups that, according to Harari's argument, overcame Homo sapiens' humanoid counterparts. But these organizations that are based on stories or myths can only survive as long as people believe.

We fear that if the group that condemns our past is successful, they will undermine and destroy the very values in society that benefit the individual. This is not to say that criticism is not important, nor that we cannot do better. We were not a perfect union in 1776—we were a more perfect union. And through thoughtful criticism and the desire to preserve the union, we created compromise, and we are better today than we were in 1776.

But certainly we have further to go. If we respect those who got us here, honor them and seek to do better, we will dramatically improve the human condition. However, we cannot give too much deference to the spirit of resentment that destroys the very society that benefits the individual. The sin of it shall be so great we cannot bear it.

We belong to something bigger, and that something is

awesome. Through free markets and individualism, we have done more to move forward the human condition than at any other time or any other place in history. This is undeniable. There is no evidence that free markets are more racist than other market types. There is significant evidence that other market types fail to improve the human condition.

Think of the statue of David. It is probable that those who worked in the quarry to find this piece of marble were oppressed. Therefore, one could decide to hate the statue for what it represents. Another approach is to appreciate the beauty and the art. This does not mean you have to support the oppression, only instead to recognize that the anger and resentment could cause you to lose the beauty of the art.

There is a significant benefit to understanding that you belong to something bigger. That what you belong to, by being an American citizen, is something to be proud of. We have accomplished what just 50 years ago would be considered incredible. American ingenuity, by any standard, has dominated the last 50 years. You can bet we will dominate the next 50, and in the process, we will make incredible improvements to the human condition.

Leave Your Moral Elitism at the Door

Paul has a story he often likes to tell. When he was a teenager, he answered the door to find a man who worked for his father. The man was dirty from head to toe, and he smelled. The guy was an ex-felon for some pretty violent crimes, which Paul knew about. When the man asked to see Paul's dad, Paul told him to wait and closed the door.

His father came out and asked who was at the door. Paul told his father who it was and that the man was still out there. His dad said, "Paul it's 110 outside, why didn't you invite him in?" As he opened the door to let the man inside, he told Paul to go get him a glass of iced tea. When the man finally left, Paul's father asked him again why he was rude to the man and had left him standing outside. Paul told his father that the man was dirty, he smelled and he was an ex-con. Paul would always repeat what his father said to him next. He said: "Paul, there is no one south of you, because if there is, then there must be someone north of you. They are just east and west, at different points on the horizon."

Every person comes with gifts. People are people. But labeling them is our way of making ourselves better than them or justifying our rude behavior. More importantly, it gives us the inability to gain the gifts others have to offer. When we label someone, we make ourselves a powerless victim and create a box around ourselves that we cannot see out of. When we see others just as people, we have more options and greater power, and we can gain the gifts others have to offer.

Think of the labels you hear, or that maybe you use as a means of making yourself morally superior. Both sides have them. Sometimes they are deeply offensive. But more often than not, they are subtle digs, designed to raise your status and lower theirs. And yet these people you are labeling, regardless of where they came from, are part of that bigger thing as well. And if we approach them with love, if we talk the language of equality, not superiority, if we listen as well as talk and try to be understanding and loving, we not only make our point more powerfully, but we make ourselves better people.

One should have ideals for themselves, and that code should include a belief that they are part of something bigger. But it should also include a belief that other people are also part of something bigger. If you leave your moral superiority aside, you can both benefit.

But it has to be we, not me.

For more on embracing a "*we, not me*" *perspective, and for a link to our* Optimistic American *podcasts, please scan the QR code above.*

19

IDEAL 7: BELIEVE IN YOU, BELIEVE IN US AND ACT WITH THAT BELIEF

On many long trips across America, my partner and I exchanged ideas, wrote and edited this book. We come from very different backgrounds. One an Arab Jew, the other a born-and-bred American; one a psychologist, the other an entrepreneur; one a dancer, the other a politician. Each of us added our thoughts and ideas, but we note that many of these ideas are lessons that we learned from reading, living and witnessing other people's lived experiences. Most of these ideas are not unique and many are not originally ours. They are a synthesis of what we learned from many who came before us and who taught, influenced and transformed us.

The central thesis that we deeply believe in is that there are lessons that we can learn from our past, from antiquity, from listening to others and from understanding those considered the outcasts or undesirables of our society. We both strongly believe in the power of the human spirit—a power that can be greater than genetics, intellect and our station in life. We both believe in the power of innovation and creation. We both believe that the power is within to change ourselves or to change the world for the better. We are both great optimists.

So learn from history—learn from the wisdom, shortfalls, greatness and failures of others. Commit to a lifetime of education to help you improve your life skills, connect with your true purpose and unique talents, be challenged to grow, practice gratitude and fortitude and contribute meaningfully to others. Believe in yourself, constantly educate yourself and believe that through this, you will improve.

The Mindset of a Creator

Hard work builds self-worth. Every job has value. Our skills help create value. And the better we are at our jobs, the higher our self-worth. The human being has to have a purpose, and while a job is not the only way, it is one of the most abundant ways.

If work builds self-worth, creatorship fulfills the human spirit. One way to be a creator is by being an entrepreneur. But being an entrepreneur is not everyone's calling. The struggles of being in business are often hard to understand. The challenge of making sales, the fear of falling short on weekly income, the terror of not making payroll. It becomes a 24/7 job, and the entrepreneur is rarely appreciated by employees, customers or family members.

But the ability to own what you create, to be in control of your own destiny and have the ability to make a difference in the lives of the people you serve is a fulfillment that an entrepreneur gains. A business is designed to solve someone else's problem. A painter brings color to a building that is lifeless without it. They find the labor, the materials, fund the work, manage the process and give recommendations on paint.

Because we, as individuals, have unlimited problems that need solving (and businesses that try to provide those solutions have their own problems that need to be solved), the amount of potential businesses is almost unlimited. But every business starts with thinking about a particular problem—and the bigger the problem, the more transformational a business can be.

Most of the big changes that will transform the human condition will be provided not by the government but by entrepreneurs. A driverless car, a cure for cancer, extending human life and maybe even going to Mars are all endeavors that will be attempted by risk-takers, people trying to solve problems previously considered unsolvable.

Our founders knew this. In the 5th and 14th Amendments to the Constitution, the due process clause protects one's right to own what they create. Through these values being placed in the Constitution, we have created one of the greatest periods of human progress in the history of the world. Regarding most issues in society, free markets are not the problem; they are the solution.

When Jefferson penned the words "life, liberty and the pursuit of happiness," he had removed the word "property" and substituted the word "happiness." We suspect he meant happiness as a substitute for meaning. It is a fair guess that he was trying to say that some people find happiness in property, but some find it in art, music, literature or any number of other things. And he was saying that the government should not have the right to deprive anyone of that happiness.

We should each be dedicated to work. For those willing to extend their work hours and face potentially unlimited stress, entrepreneurship is an option. But regardless, we all gain a benefit from both the worker and the entrepreneur. Both should be valued, but it will be creatorship that will change the world.

Put the Oxygen Mask on Yourself First

We also both believe that you are being pounded with negative messages from politicians, news media and your peers, which all causes you to lose faith. We know how hard it is to find good news and how easy it is to slip into despair. Yet, we both believe that in looking back at even recent history, the evidence is clear: the world is getting better, and the greatest threat we have is our politics.

We also believe that freedom is not a universal value, and if we are careless, we can lose our society's focus on the individual and liberty. The starting place to save Western democracy is to save the individual that it is based upon. We can all comprehend the reason why, in an airplane, we are told to put the oxygen mask on ourselves before our children. The starting place of preserving our family—our nation—is ourselves.

In a world where our politics seems upside down, where our economy and our jobs seem on edge, a world with global threats and pandemics, it is natural that you might find yourself more distracted, irritable, paranoid, less focused, more on edge, dissociated, anxious or restless. You might find your mind wandering often, reviewing and going over things without a sense of feeling productive or running in circles to find resolutions for things that seem beyond your power and control.

The fact is no one remains unaffected by the larger societal and systemic issues. But the good news is, this disruption to our lives offers us an opportunity to reflect on what matters most to us, to identify and preserve what remains sacred, to choose what to be concerned over and how to modify our perspective and act upon what we feel is imperative.

It is more important now than ever to be patient with yourself and others, to avoid multitasking and pay attention to one thing at a time. Avoid distraction when needing to focus, turn notifications off, schedule worry time, be aware of how your emotions and behaviors may be harmful and make your mental, emotional and physical health a priority. We cannot overcome great obstacles if we are burned out and worn down. Energy is a limited resource, and we need to expend it wisely.

Emily sometimes works backwards in therapy and starts with death. What would you want to be remembered for? How would you like your family, friends and social circles to talk about you? How would you live your life differently if you were given a foreshortened life expectancy? What worries or obsessions would become meaningless? What priorities would stand out? This perspective often helps people realize what regrets they have had in life and how they will choose to live more meaningfully and purposely going forward.

The stages of grief and loss often coexist with loss of control and power. These include stages of denial, anger, bargaining, depression and ultimately acceptance. Ideally, we all want to move towards the growth stage where we can be empathic with ourselves and others, obtain reliable and trusted information needed to make informed decisions for our welfare and safety, have appreciation and gratitude for what we have rather than being consumed by threat and fear and look for creative ways to optimally adapt to change.

Other issues like mortality or awareness of death can bring out the best or worst of people. There is evidence of this in charitable contributions, volunteerism, altruistic acts, prosocial behaviors and support in community. Alternatively, awareness of mortality can have a detrimental impact on mental and emotional processes. Behaviors can become driven by fear, panic, paranoia, powerlessness, loss of control and anticipatory anxiety.

In search of meaning, strength and purpose, I suggest embracing your vulnerabilities, fears and insecurities while reconstructing and redefining your self-worth and value from that space. Think about, "What do I want?" and "How do I define myself?" A breadth of resilience research comes from traumatic stress studies. Resilience is based on adaptation to adverse conditions, flexibility, self-discovery and determining creative solutions.

This is an opportunity for transformation, courage and liberation. In the past, we may have lived by self-imposed barriers or restrictions that limit our full potential and capacity. We tend to be the greatest inhibitors of our own success and development. I encourage you to confront these fears and choose who you would like to become. Holocaust survivor Viktor Frankl wrote, "When we are no longer able to change a situation—we are challenged to change ourselves."[1] We have more power within us than we may believe.

In my clinical practice, I see a significant portion of patients who suffer from imposter syndrome. This stems from the fear of being judged and it begs the question: What forms your identity? Is it status? Wealth? Physical attributes? And what are you compromising to hold onto these possessions and constructs? It also begs the question: Who determines true identity? Who gets to drive this narrative? I like to argue that while we do not live in isolation (we are social creatures, and our beliefs are informed by messaging), ultimately you get to decide what constructs you want to live your life by, as long as they do not infringe upon the safety and rights of others.

Truth is not found outside of us, it is found within. The only way to know your true self is to question and, most importantly, listen. But sometimes we must make the journey outward in order to find the answer, which can be simple yet profound. That is when wisdom develops. I am sure as you are reading this, you can think of at least one example of this in your life. I encourage you to tell someone you trust so that you can have this experience validated; you will then become more likely to search for the truth again. By doing so, you are also then giving a beautiful gift to another, so that they too can offer you a moment in their life when they had an epiphany or realization that deeply meant something.

You Can Change the World

We are not certain that any steps by individuals could have stopped Nazi Germany or the Ba'ath Party in Iraq. We have had hours of conversations with my parents and other persecuted Jews in Iraq regarding how the events of history transpired, what was happening at a local level, how they survived, their escape and their inspirational life journey. Their histories are stories of human resilience, bravery, courage, strength, perseverance, dedication and love.

What we are sure of is that what happened to my maternal grandfather, Ezoury Shamash, and other Jews, was not only the work of Saddam Hussein. It was the work of thousands of people. We are sure that as a society, the Arab people in Iraq saw themselves as victims, Jews as villains and the Ba'ath Party as the answer. We are sure that they objectified Jews, labeled them, dehumanized them. They followed a leader who told them they had been harmed. Had this been different, so would the outcomes.

Whatever the trends are today, we are certainly confronted by people on both sides who believe they are victims, see the other side as villains and feel hopeless and invisible to the elites. They objectify others. They are looking for a leader who can save them, who will see them. Wishing this away won't work. You cannot wish away mass movements.

What we can do is to understand the butterfly effect of our actions. The small things we do can affect the big things. Psychological issues affect sociological issues every bit as much as the other way around.

We can find new options. We can be creative, opportunistic and expansive. The ability to create is not limited to the social structure you live in, though there may be certain constraints. Nelson Mandela created a movement within prison; he was not limited by constraints of even loss of freedom.

Through the objectification of people, you narrow your own choices. By narrowing those choices, you move yourself towards becoming a victim or an aggressor. Perceiving oneself as a victim is a matter of choice. War always causes us to objectify people. If you hate all Arabs, you are choosing to homogenize them as a group, ignoring all the dynamic inconsistencies and differences of subgroups within.

Trauma-informed research helps us understand the globalized impacts of trauma at a group and individual level that can persist over time and across generations. The challenge with trauma is that it forces people to simplify the unexplainable and/or the undesirable. It becomes easier to say that all Arabs are evil doers, or have the capacity to harm another without compassion or remorse. The challenge in trauma is to tease apart all the nuances, complexities and even inconsistencies that make it harder to justify a one-rule assumption of the other or of another's experience.

For decades, my mother refused to talk about the deleterious effects of her experiences. But over time, and largely in the generation of this book, she has permitted herself to experience and remember some aspects of her life story which weren't all bad. These positive moments were buried deep with the pain until recently. In fact, many beautiful moments of her lived experiences in Iraq illustrated the immense selflessness and compassion of Arabs and others, the situations in which miracles occurred and the culmination of events outside of her control that ultimately led to her purpose.

My family lived through war and death, relocation as refugees, imprisonment of family members and the abduction and disappearance of my maternal grandfather Ezoury Shamash. In Hebrew, the name Shamash signifies the light that ignites others. While all these events may seem to be embedded in an ethnocultural and family historical context, they are in fact relevant for all of us today.

For more on self-belief and the creator mindset, and for a link to our Optimistic American *podcasts, please scan the QR code above.*

20

A NEW LIFE

1972—BIR GIFGAFA, SINAI, ISRAEL

When young Joseph arrived in Israel on August 25, 1971, he was 22 years old. As part of becoming an Israeli citizen, Joseph was required to join the military. It is a requirement of every Israeli and one of the factors that contributes to the cohesiveness of Israel.

Joseph was one of the older guys in boot camp. He had a deep appreciation for what he learned. In six weeks, along with more than a hundred other young men, he was trained how to march, run, shoot, throw grenades and survive the conditions of war. More importantly, he became a part of something bigger: guarding the fighter jets that were critical to Israel surviving this war.

The bunker's camouflage kept the planes out of sight. Each of the pilots had a small tent next to the plane they flew. Their jobs in the bunker revolved around getting that plane in the air, completely combat-ready, at a moment's notice.

The lights in the underground bunker were always dim inside, creating a harsh environment. Joseph's job was to march around the plane for his entire shift to make sure people followed the rules and to protect the plane from foul play. He was not, nor was anyone without clearance, permitted to exceed the boundary around the jets. One could not climb on them nor touch them. Joseph could see the tiny space for the pilot in the cockpit and wondered what it might be like to fly it, but that was as close as he could get.

Everyone knew that the base was an easy target for any foreign army that crossed into Israel. Everyone knew that their success was key to the survival of Israel. Yet for hours, some-times days, nothing happened except walking around a plane in a dark room. It was a strange mix of high anxiety and boredom.

This was juxtaposed with the occasional intensity of being in a war zone. When a call came in and the alarms rang, it became a period of extreme stress. With the sound of the alarm in the background, everyone began to rush to their stations. Pilots would jump out of a dead sleep, run to the plane, put on their gear and jump into the plane. Mechanics would conduct last-minute checks; flag men would run to their spots to direct planes out of the bunker. Then the planes would fire up. It created a loud beating sound that pounded against the men's chests. And then the jet would start to scream as it began to move, giving way to the loud *whoosh*. Men would then yell, "He is out!" as the next plane fell into position.

And as soon as it was over, it was back to extreme boredom.

Evelyn arrived in Israel on April 13, 1973 when she was only 20 years old. While she knew Joseph from Baghdad, as he was in her sister's (Claire's) class, it was not until he completed his army service that he was introduced to her through a Shidduch (a system of matchmaking in which Jewish singles are intro-duced to one another for the purpose of marriage).

In Baghdad, Evelyn's father, Ezoury Shamash, was incredibly successful. His estate, butler, maid and gardener had put his family, and thus Evelyn, in the elite of Iraqi society. They had a manicured garden, laundry taken care of and meals prepared for them. Evelyn had led a sheltered life, naive to the ways of the world. While Evelyn, her mom and two brothers were safer in Israel and tried to be grateful for what they had, the tiny apartment they now lived in represented a big fall for the Shamash family.

Ezoury, before being taken by the Ba'ath Party, had taken care of his family, and like all children, Evelyn had taken it for granted. It wasn't that she was ungrateful; she just didn't know how hard life could become. In a moment, she lost everything she knew and had to learn to confront the harshness and hostilities of life. She grew up in a loving home that was a place of refuge for herself and her family. She had no way of knowing that without the blanket of security provided by Ezoury, it would all disappear. She had no way of knowing that she might become the main provider for her family, shouldering the responsibilities for her two younger brothers and her mother.

When Evelyn, her two younger brothers and her mother left Iraq, they took nothing with them but the clothing on their backs. She left everything behind except the haunting memories, and the guilt of leaving her father and the uncertainty about what had happened to him followed her. It was an incredible sense of loss and mournful sorrow that would remain as a lingering and haunting nightmare.

Evelyn had not finished college, and she had no real skills to hold a steady job. So she did whatever she could—babysitting, teaching Arabic and other odd jobs—just to try and pay the rent and put food on the table for the family.

Evelyn had become hardened in response to these challenges and harsh realities. Yet she was still a young woman with beautiful Arabic features, curly dark hair and olive skin. Her smile could belie the anger she felt at her fellow Arabs for turning on her family. It disguised her guilt about leaving her father and her horror of losing everything that had once sheltered her from the toils of a dangerous world. That same smile could also show a glow that was more than just attractive. She had the light of purpose, a code of honor and duty that kept her always forging forward and preparing for the future.

Evelyn was preparing to welcome Joseph Bashah to her family's tiny apartment. She was not really sure about Joseph yet. He was kind enough, but she hadn't completely forgiven him for missing the first date that had been arranged for them previously by Joseph's mother and Evelyn's aunt.

On that first date, Evelyn's aunt had told Evelyn to look for a white car at the bus station. She was sending Evelyn to meet a young man who had grown up near the Shamash family in Iraq. Evelyn arrived early.

Joseph, however, did not show up in a white car. He worked for a car company and convinced his boss to allow him to take a blue Dodge Dart, which Joseph saw as a luxury car, to impress Evelyn. It resulted in the two being at the right location at the right time but unable to identify each other. It also resulted in Evelyn feeling as though she was stood up. It took some convincing to get her to go to a second rendezvous spot to meet Joseph. But she went, and Joseph was willing to pursue her.

Now, after a few meetings, Joseph was coming over to Evelyn's house. Had this meeting been in her home in Baghdad, the maids would have prepared food and cleaned the fine carpets, and Evelyn would have been left to only entertain her suitor. But there were no carpets for a maid to clean, or even a lawn for a gardener to tend. In fact, there was no food to prepare for Joseph at all.

In addition to all this, Evelyn found Joseph a bit presumptuous. He came into the home as though he owned it. She was appalled when he just went into the kitchen and opened up the fridge to see what was available to eat. It was embarrassing, as she knew the fridge was empty. And as she had come from a more refined upbringing, Joseph was taking liberties she thought revealed something lesser about Joseph's station in life.

But then Joseph said something she would never forget. He saw that there was nothing to eat or drink in the fridge and realized it was empty because Evelyn and her family did not have the money to fill it. Joseph turned to Evelyn and told her the full sum of money he made and the amount he gave to his mother every month. He told her that what amount remained, he would give to help take care of them.

Evelyn was a very proud person. She had grown up mannered. It was a gift she could not accept. But she knew at that moment, she had met a chivalrous, honest and truly good-natured man. A man who would put his needs behind the needs of others. A man who would put his needs behind his family and his children. It was his generosity and heart that she instantly fell in love with. It was genuinely Joseph's character.

From that point on, Joseph and Evelyn were destined to marry. Joseph and Evelyn were Jewish, but they were Arab Jews, and as such were accustomed to Arab culture and traditions. Their culture valued family and children, was socially conservative and did not take courting lightly. *Rahna,* or walking together, was the act of courting a woman you wanted to marry.

It is hard to understand rahna in the modern day of dating apps that offer instant connection and whatever level of intimacy each party desires, in an age where there is no courting process or formality. In Arab culture, the man had to be determined to earn the attention of a woman and not be easily intimidated by rejection. Joseph had to prove his worthiness to Evelyn, and she had to be willing to allow him to see, learn and understand her. This is the delicateness and the art of love.

In Rahna, a couple would take many, many long walks together. These walks did not have to go anywhere specific, but the couple would talk, consult and listen to each other. Through this process, they would learn about one another in depth. They would also take the time to just be together— watching the sunset, listening to the wind, holding hands and yearning to hold one another closer. Once you "go out" or walk together in this culture, a marriage is expected, and everyone knows it.

Joseph and Evelyn did exactly that. They took walks, talked and watched sunsets. They grew a love and admiration for one another. And they began planning for their wedding and to have a family.

The Yom Kippur War

On October 6th, 1973, an Arab coalition led by Egypt and Syria launched a surprise attack against Israel during Yom Kippur. The war began with Egypt crossing the Suez Canal into the Sinai Peninsula. Almost at the same time, Syria would cross the Golan Heights and push deep into Israel before Israel could prepare and launch a counter-offensive.

Young Joseph Bashah had served his time in the army and returned to a civilian job at Hertz by the time the Yom Kippur War began. For a hard-working man like Joseph, Hertz was a plum job. Joseph knew that in Israel, every man (except the Haredi Jew, whose focus on the Torah and spiritual path exempted them from mandatory service) not only enlisted in mandatory service, but that service was for life. In war, and especially a war like Yom Kippur, every man and woman is expected to serve, as failure could mean the Jews in Israel would eventually (or immediately) suffer the same fate Jews faced in Iraq.

In the book *Start-up Nation,* authors Dan Senor and Saul Singer made the case for the importance of Israel to continue commerce during the war to minimize the losses of companies that operated there. Israel was constantly under attack and if commerce and production stopped, then Israel would be a risky place to invest. Without investments, Israel would eventually be unable to sustain itself and its defense.

Hertz International had investments in Israel. The capital investment from Hertz International was through cars. And in wartime, returning your car was important to no one except Hertz and the Israeli government. Israel believed it needed to continue to produce products and to pay its debts for its long-term interest, even during the war.

Joseph was in charge of the Israel Hertz garage. He supervised three people. In the very first days of the war, Joseph's boss from India came in and told Joseph that they had cars stuck everywhere. One of the big groups not returning cars included reporters who were visiting the war front. After a reporter was deep into the front lines, if the line moved in the wrong direction, the reporter would abandon the car. Joseph was assigned the job of retrieving the cars and, if possible, getting them back into production.

Joseph's first assignment was to retrieve a car near or across the Syrian border. Joseph was being sent to Golan Heights to retrieve a car in the middle of a war zone. He could see first-hand soldiers from both sides shooting each other. He could hear bombs and actually see them exploding.

When Joseph arrived at the scene and spoke to the person in command, they could not believe he was there to retrieve a rental car. They immediately went to their commanding officer. All Joseph remembered was a proud, stout man adorned with military symbols and medals coming over to meet Joseph. After hearing the details of the car, he put out an order to find the car and return it.

Joseph went to a safe location where he could watch the activity on the roads. He could see soldiers using cars to go from place to place. He also saw them using the cars for cover

—cars they undoubtedly did not own, and neither did the Israeli government. The vehicles were battered, wrecked, full of bullet holes and some were on fire.

After sitting for a while, Joseph finally heard the loud sound of a broken muffler. He looked up and saw the orange car, windows blown out, bullet holes everywhere, smoke coming out, speeding across the war zone, back to the safety of the Israel tent. Obviously, someone was risking their life to get Joseph this car.

After Joseph thanked the soldiers for retrieving the car, he got in and drove as fast as he could away from the battlefield. He longed for safety away from the combat zone, and visions of deceased corpses continued to be a reminder of the fragility of life. Joseph safely returned the car to Haifa. He envisioned that when he arrived there and told the harrowing story of retrieving the car, he would be given time off to rest and shake off the stress of his experience with death and war. Alas, instead he was immediately assigned to pick up another car.

This time he was sent south to the other Israeli front at the Suez Canal, a waterway in Egypt connecting the Mediterranean Sea to the Red Sea through the Isthmus of Suez, dividing Africa and Asia. When Joseph got to a bridge at the Suez Canal, it was two days following General Sharon's push deep into the Sinai Peninsula. Sharon had pushed his army into Egypt and was slowly proceeding toward the town of Suez. It was one of the bloodiest conflicts of the war.

When Joseph arrived, he could see men and tanks crossing the bridge. He could see helicopters flying the wounded and dead. Buses and cars were on fire. And he could see a battle-field littered with burned bodies. He saw men wounded, disfig-ured and dead. It would haunt him for the rest of his life.

Joseph again sought out the command to tell them he was there to retrieve a Volvo rental car. Joseph remembered the guilt he felt from the look of soldiers who could not believe why he was there. But Joseph was under orders also, and the fact that he got into the war zone showed that the Israeli government saw his job as important. The soldiers began making phone calls.

Finally, one of the calls resulted in a general asking to speak to Joseph. Joseph told the general what he was sent to do. The general told Joseph to stay put. He said when the army found the car, they would get it to him.

From Joseph's vantage point, he could see the tanks and soldiers going back and forth across the bridge all night long. The traffic was heavy, and it was obvious that Israel was putting everything it had into making sure they were successful. Finally, a call came in for Joseph. The army had found the car and would bring it back across the bridge. Sometime in the early morning hours, Joseph could see a tank towing a Volvo across the bridge. He assumed it had to be his.

The Volvo was beaten to a pulp. It was riddled with bullet holes. It needed a lot of bodywork. And it didn't run. After going through the steps, Joseph figured out the car needed a pump. He was able to jerry-rig it with parts the army provided. He fixed the car and left the battlefront as quickly as he could go.

Joseph drove all night across the Sinai desert. He would have to continually pull off to the side of the road to allow the military to drive in the opposite direction, into the war zone. Joseph drove until he got the car to Bir Sheva. Then he had to get a third car in Sharm Al-Sheikh in south Sinai.

When Joseph got to that car, he found it had a broken clutch. All Joseph remembered was no shade, wide open desert, sand, rocks and heat. Without any way to jack up the car, Joseph lay on the hot sand and put the clutch back together with the transmission laid out on his chest. All he could remember was his desire to get home.

When Joseph got home, he was immediately notified that

his army unit had been activated. Even though he had served his time in the military, he was going to have to go back. As a mechanic, Joseph had seen all major fronts of the Yom Kippur War. He thought about the burned and maimed soldiers. He thought that Israel would always be under threat from the Islamic world that surrounded them.

On October 22, 1973, a ceasefire negotiated by the United Nations fell apart. The Third Army under General Sharon, which Joseph had witnessed crossing the Suez Canal in bloody conflict, had taken Suez. This would result in significant tension between the world's two superpowers, the US and the Soviet Union. On October 25th, 1973, the second ceasefire went into place and the Yom Kippur War ended.

Joseph's feelings became compounded by Evelyn, who he began courting several months after the war ended. Evelyn's experiences in Iraq had caused her to desire safety, security and stability if she was going to have a family. After Joseph and Evelyn were married, they decided to live somewhere that was not war-torn. They wanted to live in a place where they and their children would not live under the daily threat of war, oppression or terror. Joseph's and Evelyn's view was cast. They wanted something different for their children than the life they had lived in the Middle East.

On November 26th, 1974, Joseph and Evelyn were married. The wedding was held in a synagogue in Ramat Gan that specifically catered to Iraqi Jewish customs and traditions. Evelyn had spent the day by herself in the bridal beauty spa and was absolutely stunning. She had a long braided hairpiece attached to her hair, a sheer white hat, extravagant makeup and polished nails. She was dazzling in every way a bride could be. Evelyn wore the same wedding dress of her sister Ferial, the one she'd brought with her from Baghdad when she left. It was a beautiful gown that Ezoury had purchased for Ferial, adorned with embroidered flowers and pearls, handmade by famous Lebanese dressmakers. She wore the engagement ring with two diamonds that Joseph's mother had specially made from her own ring. But there was just one problem: the groom was missing.

An hour went by. Some of the family wondered if Joseph missing Evelyn on their first date foreshadowed him missing the wedding, but Evelyn knew that Joseph was an honorable man. She waited patiently, knowing that he would show up. An hour and a half after the wedding was supposed to start, Joseph arrived. He was late because he was washing the car and decorating it with flowers. Joseph wanted it to be worthy of his special bride.

Joseph and Evelyn went to Lake Kinneret in Tiberias for their honeymoon. This was the place where a Jewish man thousands of years before had walked on water and began ministries that became one of the largest religions on planet earth. Regardless of the differences of Christianity, Jews believe that a Messiah (the *Moshiach* in Hebrew, meaning savior) is coming. For Joseph and Evelyn, their savior was creating a new life, a family with children and love.

One month after the wedding, Evelyn's mother and two brothers immigrated to Montreal to join her other two brothers. On their honeymoon, Joseph and Evelyn decided to immigrate to Canada as well. A year later, on January 22nd, 1976, the couple arrived in Montreal. They arrived in the heart of winter, with temperatures reaching as low as -11 degrees Fahrenheit. They had never owned winter coats, hats, gloves or snow shoes before and this was a shock to their existence coming from the Middle East.

The two purchased a small house on the outskirts of town. Evelyn's mother and youngest brother lived with them, and they would have two children: my brother and I. Evelyn loved Canada, but the snow and having no family was tough on Joseph. Ten years later, Joseph's boss gave him a work permit to relocate to Arizona, and the Bashah family entered the US on May 1, 1985.

My parents' journey had an incredible effect on me, and I consider them my personal heroes. As the child of these two wonderful immigrants, the lessons for me are different. I was raised under the security of Western democracy in Canada and the United States. I do not have the same hurt from seeing some of my Arab friends abandon me or the terror from the Arab mobs as they clamored to hang innocent men. I did not feel the pain of my father being abducted and tortured or the guilt of having to leave him. I didn't experience the pain of leaving everything I cared about—my friends, my home, my wealth—behind for others to plunder. While I have not experienced these horrific things, my parents' journey has created an incredible impact on my worldview.

As far as the Arab community, I see them as part of my past. I am Jewish and I am an Arab. I have Arab friends. I do not hold them responsible for what happened to my parents. I do not distrust them because of prejudices they may have. In fact, I love the things that make them Arab. I love their culture, customs and traditions.

However, I have a powerful sense of injustice for any people who are oppressed. I not only think about the plight of immigrants, but I have also worked with many of them professionally to help them persevere despite the pain they have suffered. I know firsthand how they often have to leave places they love because their lives are threatened. These immigrants, like my parents, had to leave everything behind.

I have worked with people facing these issues who are Jewish, Palestinian, Latino and from other ethnic groups as well. From each of them, I have learned a lot. They have all transformed me. I know that in some way, the families of almost all Americans immigrated here looking for a better life. I believe the story of these immigrants is, in fact, our story as a country dedicated to liberty.

I believe there are incredible lessons we can learn from these immigrants. Some lessons from my parents' journey stand out to me.

Freedom is Not a Universal Value

We deeply value freedom in the United States. We tend to believe this is a universal value around the world. We think everyone wants these same basic rights that we value. But freedom is not a universal value. Power and religion are more universal than freedom. Many people around the world would give up freedom to ensure that the altar they worship at is the altar at which all people must worship. Power, and the consolidation of power, is a more important value to the men who want to lead or control people.

Even the value of freedom within the United States is not assured. There are many of our own people with competing values who would overthrow our constitutional ideals of freedom and liberty in exchange for security, religious beliefs or profit. It is clear that even here at home, freedom, civil rights, equal rights, human rights and property rights are constantly under threat. Sometimes it takes the ability to look back to understand the potential dystopian world that could be created from the loss of those freedoms.

In the United States and most Western democracies, we worship at the altar of freedom. This is one of our most important values. It is what unites us. It is why most people come here. However, Freedom House, the oldest American institution dedicated to democracy around the world, estimates that for the 13th year in a row, democracy is on the decline and authoritarian governments are on the rise. The consolidation of authoritarian regimes such as China and Russia, as well as the decline of democratic values in established democracies including the United States, has created a crisis around the world where strongman governments are on the march.

More authoritarian governments are banning opposition groups, jailing their leaders, extinguishing term limits and pressuring free media. And in the process, corrupt political appointees like the ones who took everything Ezoury owned are empowered to abuse citizens and line them up with corrupt influences. This is happening both in the retreat of Western democratic values in government and in the corruption that is allowed to exist through oligarchs or drug cartels. It is putting a squeeze on freedom.

As that squeeze expands, it will put increasing pressure on Western democracies. People who want to worship at that same altar of freedom, people who want liberty and those who are oppressed will fight hard to come to places like the United States. They come here because the United States has stood as a beacon of those values. While I am a supporter of immigrant rights, I do believe that we need to make sure that people coming to the US believe in this same value. But we will have to choose if we even want to continue to be that sanctuary we have represented for so long. We certainly hope that we do.

The Human Rights Debate

Regardless, this squeeze will make the United States evaluate if it is still committed to its core values. The first and most important value that Thomas Jefferson stated in the Declaration of Independence, long before the Constitution was drafted, is:

"We hold these truths to be self-evident, that all men are created equal. They are endowed upon by their creator with certain inalienable rights." We are facing a test of these original concepts. Do we believe that God gave all people inalienable rights, or do we believe that those rights can be taken from an individual and are only valid if you are a citizen?

In the US, we have had a civil rights debate and an equal rights debate—and we have just begun to debate human rights. Do we extend those inalienable rights to those immigrants who come here legally and illegally? Do we believe they deserve due process, humane treatment and safety? Or are those rights we espouse not available to them?

American Jews spent significant resources trying to help Jews in places like Iraq. Operation Ezra and Nehemiah airlifted out between 130,000 to 150,000 Jews.[1] The name Ezra and Nehemiah refers to those in the Hebrew Bible who helped Jews who were exiled from Babylon return to Israel in the 5th century BCE. Jews like myself would never have even been born without the help of those Americans who aided people like my parents. However, history tells us they could have done more for the Jews who were persecuted. We visit Holocaust museums, but do we understand the weight of a story like the MS St. Louis, where 900 Jewish refugees on a passenger ship were first denied visas in Cuba, denied asylum in the US and finally sent back to the horrors of the Holocaust from which they had fled? Many of them did not survive. How could the United States allow that to happen? In fact, we are doing this very same thing today.

I was blessed to be raised under the blanket of freedom that the United States offers me, but I believe from my family's story that we have a human obligation to everyone facing the same oppression and terror that my parents faced.

My parents' lives led me into service, where I have the honor to work with people who have suffered immense grievances by foreign governments, resulting in them taking on Herculean tasks in search of a better life. In contrast, forensic work has taught me about the personal nuances and contextual factors that may shape and influence distortions of the mind and perceptions of defendants charged with terrorism or first-degree murder. All of these vast and different experiences further enrich my appreciation for and foster a better understanding of humanity at large.

21

FATE VERSUS DESTINY

My client was partly silhouetted by the floor-to-ceiling glass window. Below me outside was a runway for airplanes bound for destinations unknown. As I listened to my client, I thought about all the things that I had learned and the many people I had worked with around the globe.

The client had come to talk about being a victim. However, the client was beginning to cross the line from talking about his problems to seeing me as his oppressor.

The young man was large, malodorous and disheveled. This all belied the good family that he had come from. He was paranoid, angry and loud. He was also growing agitated that his father was late to pick him up. I knew the session had to conclude quickly.

It was still fresh in my mind that just months before, a man had killed a prominent forensic psychiatrist, paralegals and others who he had viewed as oppressors—those who had been involved in a court case of his. In June of 2018, Dwight Lamon Jones murdered forensic psychiatrist Steven Pitt, who had provided a risk assessment of Jones a decade earlier. The assessment concluded that Jones was going to continue to be a danger, and without psychiatric intervention, he would become increasingly paranoid, likely psychotic and pose an even greater risk for perpetrating violence. When Jones was released, he fulfilled that prediction not far from my office, killing Pitt and five others.[1]

As the young man became more agitated, I called his father and urged him to come as soon as he could. The client's thought process was disorganized and disjointed, and his speech was incoherent. His rants included conspiracy theories seemingly tied to an unintelligible ideology. As I tried to escort him downstairs, he turned towards the backroom and went into the kitchen, shuffling through drawers in search of a knife. From the records I reviewed, I knew this was his typical response when feeling threatened. But I knew the dangers. Somehow, with the assistance of my postdoctoral resident, we were able to redirect him and safely escort him outside of the building and to his father.

I went back into my office for a few moments and watched the planes land and depart. I tried to focus on what had just happened. Staring out the window, watching those planes, my mind drifted to the tragedy and despair I had seen up close in people's lives. It is human nature to try to find something or someone to blame when confronted with problems that do not have clear solutions. In blaming some external source or creating some kind of scapegoat, we may feel temporary relief, but the problem remains or is exacerbated.

In many, many cases, much larger than the list of stories I recounted in this book, people I have worked with have had challenges that make it difficult for them to find a place in society in which they feel they are valued and belong. The challenges they faced may have genetic, neuropsychological or biological origins, but nurture is another large influencing factor.

I thought of the struggles of the victims, the accused, the gentle giant, the immigrants and my mother and father and all that they endured and heroically overcame. I thought about them and so many other people whose struggles and traumas had massive effects on their lives. Some of these people may be beyond the help of this book, or any book for that matter. So many others created terrible circumstances for themselves and the people who loved them, one step at a time. For them, different decisions would have resulted in a dramatically different life.

There is a difference between fate and destiny. Destiny is uncontrollable, out of our hands and possibly preordained. Maybe, I thought staring out the window, both special and horrific events in life are pre-determined, established by events that we have no control over. But for so many others, our fate is something we play a role in determining. The decisions we make have huge long-term effects on our lives. And these effects last long after the decisions are made.

There is also a fine line that exists between sociology and psychology. Psychology is the study of the human mind, mental constructs, psychosocial influences, emotional processes and behavior. Sociology, on the other hand, is the accumulation of thousands of those minds into a societal architecture and the trends that follow. But for Paul and I, these things are tied together. History, psychology, politics and our stories are inter-woven. And we can affect the outcome.

In Baghdad during the 1970s, a society driven by the Ba'ath Party had determined that Jews were undesirable. They had created an environment, by controlling the means of communi-cation, that made it appear that Jews were an alien culture responsible for the damage that so many people felt in the Arab world.

My parents and my grandparents had no real control over these global trends, but they still had choices. Even after being ostracized, objectified and imprisoned, they had choices. My mother, father and ancestors chose to survive, preserve their family lineage, live courageously and humbly, preserve what was most sacred, pass on their enriched identity and celebrate their Judaism. Their lives have continued toward prosperity, and their legacy is their victory in the face of attempted genocide, annihilation and oppression.

In our American society, many of those "undesirable" labels are focused on immigrants, minorities or people with addictions. For many of the people in these aggrieved communities, this construct has caused struggle and trauma. Yet again, these people have choices: to remain a victim and blame the system which has imposed this subjugation or to rise above the construct and meaningfully engage in an empowering social movement.

In our society, we are bombarded with negative messages— from our politicians, the nightly news, the newspapers and oftentimes from one another. It is easy to view the world as being out of control, in regression and moving in the wrong direction.

Yet we can choose another view—one that recognizes great optimism. A worldview that in the evolution of society, one cannot deny that the lot of the average person has dramatically improved—not only for the last thousand years, but in the last 50. Literacy rates have been improving, living conditions have been improving and the buying power of the average person is improving. There is significant evidence, oftentimes ignored, that the world is doing demonstrably better than what one might assume from the news cycle.

I have found that, over and again, the people who I have worked with yearn for that optimism. They have loved the stories of people who have struggled mightily, lived bravely and overcame adversity. It gives them pause and purpose, and it makes them grateful for their own lives. My role as a psychologist, at times, is to offer my clients tools to cope with trauma, struggles, losses and mental health challenges.

I have used the drama triangle[2] to show how the victim, the persecutor and the savior were all three trapped in their dilemma, and the only way out is through. This means that through exploring and expanding one's options and choices, the cycle can be broken. Oftentimes, I find that people become so entrapped in their dilemma that the construct becomes an integral part of their own identity, and seeing anything beyond it is too perplexing and feels impossible to overcome.

Conversely, damage and dysfunction persist by objectifying others. The labels we place on others can keep people living in their own bubbles, which perpetuates harm. I have offered lessons like "every day begins new," "begin with love," and "master your emotions." These are intended to assist people in coping with life's challenges and help them navigate difficult conditions, regardless of the situation that they find themselves in.

But most importantly, I have found, at least in my own life, that gratitude is an essential ingredient for happiness. In my travels, work and experiences, I have met people who have suffered unbelievable and untold injustices. I have listened to their stories, in awe of how they could have possibly survived and remained to have the courage to continue in life. For those people who have not only survived but thrived, I found some common ingredients: having optimism about tomorrow, gratitude for today, creating meaning from suffering and having the strength and persistence to keep going.

My parents, after their family members were abducted, jailed, tortured, terrorized and murdered, fled with nothing but the clothes on their backs, and they still had hope and gratitude for their lives. They also developed a survival mentality that extended to others within the tribe. There is a shared meaning, belonging, connection and coexistence. It is just as important to help and assist others in the tribe, even if it means neglecting one's own needs. This value is sadly dying in American culture, as I witness more people focusing on their own hedonistic pleasures and in constant competition to get ahead or above one another, even if it means pulling others down to get above them. There is a metaphor depicting "a bucket of crabs mentality"[3] which highlights that people who strive to pull others down also hurt themselves because they miss the opportunities that cooperation and collaboration provide.

Gentle Jim, who was in prison for murder most likely for the rest of his life, found gratitude in being able to help other people. Immigrants, who had given up everything they owned for a passageway into the United States, often escaped cartels and other forms of violence in search of the promise and hope for a better future only to find themselves being deported. Even they often found gratitude, hope and perseverance. These men, women and children embody the definition of resilience.

Over and over again, I meet people who have experienced similar traumas and tragedies, who through hope, faith and gratitude found a better life. I also meet many people whose life conditions coupled with their worldview construct keep them in the victim trap.

These people become highly susceptible to leaders and politicians who want to manipulate them. They often alienate their friends, their children and even their families. And in some cases, they find themselves in prison, believing that all hope is lost.

I admit that it is easier for me to be grateful for my family, my life, my safety, my stability and even my comfort after hearing so many tragic stories. I recognize my privileges, my rights as a woman in this country, my ability to pursue a doctorate degree and my independence. I would not be able to do any of these as a Jewish woman born in Iraq, to have the ability to choose my path in life. I know what the alternative existence is, and it perplexes me when Americans justify exercising their right to refute democracy, seeming to forget how their ancestors fought, died and sacrificed for that very right.

Along with doing my psychology work, every now and then, I put on my belly-dancing garb, with layered coins and gems, and dance in front of an unsuspecting audience. I listen to their stories about their lives and their families. I listen to their struggles as Jews, Arabs, Palestinians, other minorities and, at times, just people who yearn for a connection to their homeland and reminiscence of where they came from.

They have no idea when I'm dancing that I am a Jew whose ancestors were tortured, murdered and exiled. They have no idea that I am the mother of a beautiful young girl. They have no idea that I am a trained psychologist. I am grateful for the ability to do this work, to preserve a sacred part of humanity. We are all connected despite our varying paths. There is optimism even in the worst conditions. Escaping addictive ideologies is the only road to enjoying the many gifts life has to offer.

POST SCRIPT

בִּרְכַּת שֶׁהֶחֱיָינוּ
בָּרוּךְ אַתָּה יְיָ
אֱלֹהֵינוּ מֶלֶךְ הָעוֹלָם
שֶׁהֶחֱיָינוּ וְקִיְּמָנוּ
וְהִגִּיעָנוּ לַזְּמַן הַזֶּה:

Hebrew Blessing: Who Has Given Us Life
Blessed are you, Adonai,
Source of all life,
who has sustained us, and kept us alive,
and brought us to this time.

On a freezing morning in February 2022, after months of military buildup on Ukraine's borders, Vladimir Putin announced his invasion of Ukraine. During the buildup, Putin repeatedly told the world he had no intent to invade. After finding his effort stalled, he turned the vacuum rockets and cluster bombs to apartment complexes, cultural facilities and civilians themselves. It reminded the world that the line between authoritarianism and totalitarianism is a thin one indeed.

Five days before the invasion, Paul and I celebrated our daughter's first birthday. Her party had a theme from Babylon, representing her past and ancestors. Jewish members of our family came to bestow gifts. To them, Adinah is a survivor of the genocide perpetrated by the Ba'ath Party against Jews and other dissidents in Iraq. She is their legacy of survival.

In the coming months on the nightly news, we saw the bravery of young Ukrainian boys going back home to fight for freedom. We saw President Volodymyr Zelenskyy not abandon his post, even when he knew his family's very lives stood in the balance. We watched as millions of people, mostly women and children, fled as refugees with nothing but the clothing on their backs, hoping only that their children would have a future. Their only prayer was to be among the lucky survivors.

During Saddam Hussein's rule in Iraq, there were no Jewish survivors among those who stayed. There were only survivors for those fortunate enough to find their way out—and only then because Israel made their survival a priority.

The values passed on to me by survivors, and now to my daughter, are not the values of being a victim. Being a victim, one must relive and remain in the pains of the past. One must allow persecutors to continue to play a role in their life. One must subordinate everything of value, mainly the future, to the dark hauntings of their past. With my parents, I witnessed people who had lost everything—their fortunes, family members' lives and even their dignity. Yet they found strength to start over, to start with nothing and to build a life with their children and those who would come after.

My daughter Adinah is a recipient of those values. She has a rich history of traditions, wisdom and heritage. She is raised to know where she comes from and to be proud of her background. The legacy continues with her.

The similar thread that I witness in my parents, in refugees and in people who have spent their lives in prison is, in fact, a mindset. One mindset is to remain a victim: vengeful, resentful, fearful and bitter. An alternative mindset could be to begin anew with courage, regardless of feeling defeated. These lessons are important. They are the lessons I hope to teach my daughter. To understand the struggle that existed in her grandparents' escapes from genocide by the Ba'ath Party and the struggle for freedom that is very much alive today. To recognize that others who perished did not die in vain. Their courage, strength and dedication to fighting for freedom and our right to exist are palpable. Their efforts must be recognized and celebrated.

Being a psychologist gives me the opportunity to help other people by promoting healing and social justice and allows me to further see the shared humanity in mankind. Paul's involvement in business and politics has allowed me to witness and understand how psychology would apply to the masses in sociology. We hope this book helps others understand their own opportunities to improve their lives and uncover their own hidden truths.

As for my dance, it keeps me connected to something deeper inside of me. Its ancient moves and garb remind me that I am part of something bigger. Though it brings me joy, I am starkly aware of the stereotypes that some people place on belly dancing. However, joy and hardship are eternally linked.

No great art nor great accomplishment happens with universal applause. Sometimes it is a quiet whisper inside the artist. I love the quote of the famous 13th century Sufi philosopher Jalal ad-Din Muhammad Rumi: "Dance when you're broken open. Dance if you've torn the bandage off. Dance in the middle of the fighting. Dance in your blood. Dance when you're perfectly free."

ACKNOWLEDGMENTS

We want to acknowledge the contributions made to this book by our families, people who believed in us, our teachers, professors, mentors and spiritual leaders who have contributed so much to our understanding of human nature and appreciation of life's incredible journey. We hope this book honors all the gifts that they have given us.

We specifically want to acknowledge the contribution of Evelyn and Joseph Bashah, in honor of their courageous efforts in escaping persecution from the brutal Ba'ath Party in Iraq. As ethnic minority (Jewish-Iraqi) immigrants, they struggled for a better life for their children in Canada and America. They fought to preserve and protect those values they held most sacred. Along with the stories of their other family members, their personal stories of escape, sacrifice and survival transcend oppression and persecution. Their will to transform trauma into a celebration of life is an inspiration to us all.

ABOUT THE AUTHORS

Dr. Emily Bashah is an author and licensed psychologist with a private practice in Scottsdale, Arizona. An expert witness in criminal, immigration and civil courts, she has worked on high-profile cases covering issues of domestic terrorism, capital offenses and first-degree murder.

Dr. Bashah was awarded the Society for the Psychological Study of Social Issues Policy Fellowship and served within the American Psychological Association's Public Interest Government Relations Office in Washington, DC. A frequent expert guest in media, Dr. Bashah clinically specializes in mental illness, personal and collective trauma, addiction, grief and loss as well as family and relationship dynamics.

Hon. Paul E. Johnson Jr. is the host of *The Optimistic Amer-*

ican podcast, whose goal is to create space in the news media for a positive and hopeful view of America. He has a significant background in business, politics and government and became the youngest mayor of Phoenix, Arizona at 30 years old. He has managed several state campaigns for presidential candidates and is the CEO and co-founder of Redirect Health.

Emily and Paul's collaboration in life and work marries their combined skills and backgrounds in clinical and forensic psychology, politics and geopolitical issues. They address the problems of addictive ideologies to the self and to society while offering insight and wisdom for healing, growth and transformation. They believe collaborating towards a worthy purpose is essential to unleashing the power of the human spirit.

BIBLIOGRAPHY

Foreword: The Dance

1. Belly Dance by Sasha. (2019, September 12). *A history of belly dancing.* Belly Dance by Sasha. https://www.bellydancebysasha.com/belly-dancer-about-sasha/the-belly-dance/
2. Iacono, V. L. (2022, January 27). *Samia Gamal – Star of Egyptian cinema.* worldbellydance.com. https://www.worldbellydance.com/samia-gamal/

Introduction: "Who Am I?"

1. Dalio, R. (2021). *Principles for dealing with the changing world order: Why nations succeed and fail.* Simon & Schuster.
2. Hoffer, E. (1951). *The true believer: Thoughts on the nature of mass movements.* Harper.
3. Cox, D. A. (2022, February 9). *Emerging trends and enduring patterns in American family life.* The Survey Center on American Life. https://www.americansurveycenter.org/research/emerging-trends-and-enduring-patterns-in-american-family-life/
4. Boston Women's Workforce Council. (2022). *2021 Gender and racial wage gap data analysis.* https://d279m997dpfwgl.cloudfront.net/wp/2021/12/BWWC-2021-Annual-Report-Data.pdf
5. Rose, S. (2017, June 19). *White working-class men in a changing American workforce.* Third Way. https://www.thirdway.org/report/white-working-class-men-in-a-changing-american-workforce
6. Krupnikov, Y., & Ryan, J. B. (2022). *The other divide.* Cambridge University Press.

1. The Hangings

1. Sephardi Voices Team. (2020, October 2). *Remembering the hangings in Iraq.* Sephardi Voices UK. https://www.sephardivoices.org.uk/post/2019-02-15-remembering-the-hangings-in-iraq
2. Two boys were hanged, Daoud Heskel Dalal (16), a student in Basra was forced to say that he was nineteen years old so that he could be tried and

be sentenced to death and Hesqal Saleh Hesqel (17), a student from Basra was forced to say that he was over eighteen in order to be hanged

3. Fukuyama, F. (2018). *Identity: The demand for dignity and the politics of resentment*. Farrar, Straus and Giroux.

4. Praying for a Miracle

1. Haney, C., Banks, W. C., & Zimbardo, P. G. (1973). Study of prisoners and guards in a simulated prison. *Naval Research Reviews, 9* (1-17)

2. Le Texier, T. (2019). Debunking the Stanford prison experiment. *American Psychologist, 74*(7), 823–839. https://doi.org/10.1037/amp0000401

3. Milgram, S. (1963). Behavioral study of obedience. *The Journal of Abnormal and Social Psychology, 67*(4), 371–378. https://doi.org/10.1037/h0040525

4. Milgram, S. (2009). *Obedience to authority: An experimental view*. Harper-Collins.

5. Chappell, B. (2017, August 17). *Psychologists behind CIA "Enhanced interrogation" program settle detainees' lawsuit*. NPR.org. https://www.npr.org/sections/thetwo-way/2017/08/17/544183178/psychologists-behind-cia-enhanced-interrogation-program-settle-detainees-lawsuit

6. McLaughlin, E. (2018, August 26). *McCain's experience as POW shaped lifelong opposition to torture*. ABC News. https://abcnews.go.com/Politics/mccains-experience-pow-shaped-lifelong-opposition-torture/story?id=57384448

7. Aviv, E. (2016, November 28). *Millet system in the Ottoman Empire*. Oxford Bibliographies. https://www.oxfordbibliographies.com/view/document/obo-9780195390155/obo-9780195390155-0231.xml

8. History.com Editors. (2017, November 3). *Ottoman Empire*. HISTORY. https://www.google.com/amp/s/www.history.com/.amp/topics/middle-east/ottoman-empire

9. Bélanger, J. J. (2021). The sociocognitive processes of ideological obsession: review and policy implications. *Philosophical Transactions of the Royal Society B: Biological Sciences, 376*(1822), 20200144. https://doi.org/10.1098/rstb.2020.0144

5. It Was Already Too Late

1. Jewish Virtual Library. (n.d.). *Operation Ezra & Nehemia - The airlift of Iraqi Jews*. https://www.jewishvirtuallibrary.org/operation-ezra-and-nehemia-the-airlift-of-iraqi-jews

2. Total immigration of Jews to Israel from Iraq since 1948 totaled 131,065. Operation Ezra & Nehemiah, also known as Operation Ali Baba, was the

airlift of more than 120,000 Jews from Iraq to Israel shortly after the founding of the Jewish state. Retrieved from https://www.jewishvirtualli brary.org/operation-ezra-and-nehemia-the-airlift-of-iraqi-jews

6. They Took Him on His Daughter's Wedding Day

1. U.S. Department of State. (1978, October 31). *Intelligence Memorandum: Government In Iraq.* U.S. Department of State. Retrieved December 9, 2022, from https://history.state.gov/historicaldocuments/frus1977-80v18/d134
2. Morad, T., & Shasha, D. (2008). *Iraq's last Jews: Stories of daily life, upheaval, and escape from modern Babylon.* Palgrave Macmillan.

8. My Father, Joseph Bashah

1. History.com Editors. (2009, November 9). *Code of Hammurabi.* HISTORY. https://www.history.com/topics/ancient-history/hammurabi
2. Jewish Virtual Library. (n.d.). *Nebuzaradan.* https://www.jewishvirtualli brary.org/nebuzaradan-2
3. Beizer, M. (2017, July 25). *American Jewish joint distribution committee.* YIVO Encyclopedia of Jews in Eastern Europe. https://www.yivoencyclopedia. org/article.aspx/American_Jewish_Joint_Distribution_Committee
4. Szulc, T. (1991). *The secret alliance: The extraordinary story of the rescue of the Jews since World War II.* Farrar, Straus and Giroux.

10. When Home Disappears

1. At the request of family members, we have not disclosed some names to this story. Each family member have their own reason for keeping their identity undisclosed. Some family members still believe that being iden- tified creates a potential risk to their lives and the lives of their family. The trauma was so great that some still feel they live in the same risk today.
2. Diamandis, P. H., & Kotler, S. (2012). *Abundance: The future is better than you think.* Simon & Schuster.
3. *Kurdish history.* (2019, September 9). The Kurdish Project. https://thekur dishproject.org/history-and-culture/kurdish-history/

11. An American Islamic Radicalization

1. Schuurman, B., Grol, P., & Flower, S. (2016). Converts and Islamist terrorism: An introduction. *Terrorism and Counter-Terrorism Studies*. https://doi.org/10.19165/2016.2.03

2. Schuurman, B., Grol, P., & Flower, S. (2016). Converts and Islamist terrorism: An introduction. *Terrorism and Counter-Terrorism Studies*. https://doi.org/10.19165/2016.2.03

3. Jones, S. G., Doxsee, C., & Harrington, N. (2020, June 17). *The escalating terrorism problem in the United States*. Center for Strategic and International Studies. https://www.csis.org/analysis/escalating-terrorism-problem-united-states

4. George Washington University. (2021). *Anarchist/left-wing violent extremism in America: Trends in radicalization, recruitment, and mobilization*. Program on Extremism. https://extremism.gwu.edu/sites/g/files/zaxdzs2191/f/Anarchist%20-%20Left-Wing%20Violent%20Extremism%20in%20America.pdf

5. Byman, D. L. (2022, March 9). *Assessing the right-wing terror threat in the United States a year after the January 6 insurrection*. Brookings. https://www.brookings.edu/blog/order-from-chaos/2022/01/05/assessing-the-right-wing-terror-threat-in-the-united-states-a-year-after-the-january-6-insurrection/

6. O'Leary, M. (2021, November 1). *Competing visions of America: An evolving identity or a culture under attack?* PRRI. https://www.prri.org/press-release/competing-visions-of-america-an-evolving-identity-or-a-culture-under-attack/?src=newsroom

7. Lynch, S. N. (2022, January 11). *U.S. Justice Department forming unit to counter domestic terrorism*. Reuters. https://www.reuters.com/legal/government/us-justice-department-forming-unit-counter-domestic-terrorism-2022-01-11/

8. Greene, R. (2017, December 18). *Is Donald Trump mentally ill? 3 professors of psychiatry ask President Obama to conduct "A full medical and neuropsychiatric evaluation."* HuffPost. https://www.huffpost.com/entry/is-donald-trump-mentally_b_13693174/amp

9. Hannah, G., Clutterbuck, L., & Rubin, J. (2008). Radicalization or rehabilitation: Understanding the challenge of extremist and radicalized prisoners. *RAND Technical Report*. https://www.rand.org/pubs/technical_reports/TR571.html

10. Hannah, G., Clutterbuck, L., & Rubin, J. (2008). Radicalization or rehabilitation: Understanding the challenge of extremist and radicalized prisoners. *RAND Technical Report*. https://www.rand.org/pubs/technical_reports/TR571.html

11. Rabasa, A. M., Benard, C., Chalk, P., Fair, C. C., Karasik, T., Lal, R., Lesser, I., & Thaler, D. (2004). *The Muslim world after 9/11*. RAND Corporation.

13. Ideal 1: Know the Truth

1. Clarke, D. M. (2005). *Descartes's theory of mind*. United Kingdom: Clarendon Press.
2. Palmer, C. (2021, June 1). *The science of morality*. American Psychological Association. https://www.apa.org/monitor/2021/06/lab-science-morality
3. Meltzoff, A. N. (2007). The 'like me' framework for recognizing and becoming an intentional agent. *Acta Psychologica, 124*(1), 26–43. https://doi.org/10.1016/j.actpsy.2006.09.005
4. Goleman, D. (2006). *Emotional intelligence: Why it can matter more than IQ*. Bantam.
5. Gabriel, E. T., Oberger, R., Schmoeger, M., Deckert, M., Vockh, S., Auff, E., & Willinger, U. (2019). Cognitive and affective Theory of Mind in adolescence: developmental aspects and associated neuropsychological variables. *Psychological Research, 85*(2), 533–553. https://doi.org/10.1007/s00426-019-01263-6
6. Bélanger, J. J. (2021). The sociocognitive processes of ideological obsession: Review and policy implications. *Philosophical Transactions of the Royal Society B: Biological Sciences, 376*(1822), 20200144. https://doi.org/10.1098/rstb.2020.0144
7. Henderson, E. B. (2021, February 23). *New research explores why people ultimately engage in ideological violence*. News-Medical.net. https://www.news-medical.net/news/20210222/New-research-explores-why-people-ultimately-engage-in-ideological-violence.aspx
8. Blades, R. (2021). Protecting the brain against bad news. *Canadian Medical Association Journal, 193*(12), E428–E429. https://doi.org/10.1503/cmaj.1095928
9. Johnston, W. M., & Davey, G. C. L. (1997). The psychological impact of negative TV news bulletins: The catastrophizing of personal worries. *British Journal of Psychology, 88*(1), 85–91. https://doi.org/10.1111/j.2044-8295.1997.tb02622.x
10. Blades, R. (2021). Protecting the brain against bad news. *Canadian Medical Association Journal, 193*(12), E428–E429. https://doi.org/10.1503/cmaj.1095928
11. Mens, M. G., Scheier, M. F., & Carver, C. S. (2021). Optimism. In C. R. Snyder, S. J. Lopez, L. M. Edwards, & S. C. Marques (Eds.), *The Oxford handbook of positive psychology* (pp. 396–412). Oxford University Press.
12. Blades, R. (2021). Protecting the brain against bad news. *Canadian Medical Association Journal, 193*(12), E428–E429. https://doi.org/10.1503/cmaj.1095928
13. Gehl, K. M., & Porter, M. E. (2020). *The politics industry: How political innovation can break partisan gridlock and save our democracy*. Harvard Business

Press.

14. *Founders online: From Thomas Jefferson to Francis Hopkinson, 13 March 1789.* (n.d.). Founders Online, National Archives. https://founders.archives.gov/documents/Jefferson/01-14-02-0402

15. Hamilton, A., Madison, J., & Jay, J. (2009). Federalist No. 51. *The Federalist Papers*, 119–122. https://doi.org/10.1057/9780230102019_20

16. Diamandis, P. H., & Kotler, S. (2012). *Abundance: The future is better than you think.* Simon & Schuster.

17. Beckley, M. (2018). *Unrivaled: Why America will remain the world's sole superpower.* Cornell University Press.

18. Brands, H., & Beckley, M. (2021, September 24). *China is a declining power —and that's the problem.* Foreign Policy. https://foreignpolicy.com/2021/09/24/china-great-power-united-states/

19. U.S. Department of the Treasury. (2019, August 5). *Treasury designates China as a currency manipulator.* https://home.treasury.gov/news/press-releases/sm751

20. Zeihan on Geopolitics. (2022, June 14). *The end of the world is just the beginning maps.* https://zeihan.com/end-of-the-world-maps/

21. United Nations. (n.d.). *Will robots and AI cause mass unemployment? Not necessarily, but they do bring other threats.* https://www.un.org/en/desa/will-robots-and-ai-cause-mass-unemployment-not-necessarily-they-do-bring-other

22. *Global Wealth Report 2022 – record wealth growth in 2021 tapered by challenging 2022 market environment.* (2022, September 20). Credit Suisse. https://www.credit-suisse.com/about-us-news/en/articles/media-releases/global-wealth-report-2022---record-wealth-growth-in-2021-tapered-202209.html

14. Ideal 2: Your Uniqueness Entitles You to the Right to Begin Anew

1. Teigen, A. (2021, May 12). *Miller v. Alabama and juvenile life without parole laws.* National Conference of State Legislatures. https://www.ncsl.org/research/civil-and-criminal-justice/miller-v-alabama-and-juvenile-life-without-parole-laws.aspx

2. Rovner, J. (2022, September 27). *Juvenile life without parole: An overview – The sentencing project.* The Sentencing Project. https://www.sentencingproject.org/policy-brief/juvenile-life-without-parole-an-overview/

3. Grisso, T., & Kavanaugh, A. (2016). Prospects for developmental evidence in juvenile sentencing based on Miller v. Alabama. *Psychology, Public Policy, and Law, 22*(3), 235–249. https://doi.org/10.1037/law0000090

4. Teigen, A. (2021, May 12). *Miller v. Alabama and juvenile life without parole laws.* National Conference of State Legislatures. https://www.ncsl.org/

research/civil-and-criminal-justice/miller-v-alabama-and-juvenile-life-without-parole-laws.aspx

5. Brintlinger, A. (2018, December). *Alexander Solzhenitsyn*. Origins. https://origins.osu.edu/milestones/december-2018-solzhenitsyn-gulag-ussr-stalin-nobel?language_content_entity=en

6. Zimbardo, P. G. (1999). *Stanford prison experiment: A simulation study on the psychology of imprisonment*. Stanford Prison Experiment. https://www.prisonexp.org/

7. Zimbardo, P. G. (1999). *Stanford prison experiment: A simulation study on the psychology of imprisonment*. Stanford Prison Experiment. https://www.prisonexp.org/

8. Haney, C., Banks, W. C., & Zimbardo, P. G. (1973). A study of prisoners and guards in a simulated prison. *Naval Research Review*, 30, 4-17.

9. Zimbardo, P., & Boyd, J. (2008). *The time paradox: The new psychology of time that will change your life*. Simon & Schuster.

10. Pounsford, M. (2018, May 16). *Mission v purpose v vision v strategy v values?* https://couravel.com/mission-v-purpose-v-vision-v-strategy-v-values/

15. Ideal 3: Meaning Over Happiness

1. The Editors of Encyclopaedia Britannica. (2022, September 9). *Aleksandr Isayevich Solzhenitsyn*. Encyclopedia Britannica. https://www.britannica.com/biography/Aleksandr-Solzhenitsyn

2. Ericson, E. E., Jr, Solzhenitsyn, A. I., Whitney, T. P., & Willetts, H. (1985). *The gulag archipelago 1918-1956 abridged: An experiment in literary investigation* (1st ed.). HarperCollins.

3. Lieblich, J., & Boskailo, E. (2012). *Wounded I am more awake: Finding meaning after terror*. Vanderbilt University Press.

4. Kaufman, S. B. (2020, June 29). *Unraveling the mindset of Victimhood*. Scientific American. https://www.scientificamerican.com/article/unraveling-the-mindset-of-victimhood/

5. Sykes, C. J. (1992). *A nation of victims: The decay of the American character*. St Martins Press.

6. Kaufman, S. B. (2020, June 29). *Unraveling the mindset of Victimhood*. Scientific American. https://www.scientificamerican.com/article/unraveling-the-mindset-of-victimhood/

7. Karpman, S. (1968). Fairy tales and script drama analysis. *Transactional Analysis Bulletin*, 7(26), 39-43.

8. Emerald, D. (2015). *The power of ted: The empowerment dynamic*. Polaris Publishing.

9. Emerald, D. (2011, March 5). *Drama-Triangle-The-Empowerment-Dynamic*. Wikimedia Commons. https://commons.wikimedia.org/wiki/File:Drama-Triangle-The-Empowerment-Dynamic.jpg

16. Ideal 4: Leverage Yourself

1. Lukianoff, G., & Haidt, J. (2018). *The coddling of the American mind: How good intentions and bad ideas are setting up a generation for failure.* Penguin Publishing Group.
2. Celniker, J. B., Ringel, M. M., Nelson, K., & Ditto, P. H. (2022). Correlates of "Coddling": Cognitive distortions predict safetyism-inspired beliefs, belief that words can harm, and trigger warning endorsement in college students. *Personality and Individual Differences, 185,* 111243. https://doi.org/10.1016/j.paid.2021.111243
3. Celniker, J. B., Ringel, M. M., Nelson, K., & Ditto, P. H. (2022). Correlates of "Coddling": Cognitive distortions predict safetyism-inspired beliefs, belief that words can harm, and trigger warning endorsement in college students. *Personality and Individual Differences, 185,* 111243. https://doi.org/10.1016/j.paid.2021.111243
4. Moss, J., & O'Connor, P. J. (2020). The dark triad traits predict authoritarian political correctness and alt-right attitudes. *Heliyon, 6*(7), e04453. https://doi.org/10.1016/j.heliyon.2020.e04453
5. Kaufman, S. B., Yaden, D. B., Hyde, E., & Tsukayama, E. (2019). The light vs. dark triad of personality: Contrasting two very different profiles of human nature. *Frontiers in Psychology, 10, 467.* https://doi.org/10.3389/fpsyg.2019.00467
6. Moss, J., & O'Connor, P. J. (2020). The dark triad traits predict authoritarian political correctness and alt-right attitudes. *Heliyon, 6*(7), e04453. https://doi.org/10.1016/j.heliyon.2020.e04453
7. Sanz-García, A., Gesteira, C., Sanz, J., & García-Vera, M. P. (2021). Prevalence of psychopathy in the general adult population: A systematic review and meta-analysis. *Frontiers in Psychology, 12.* https://doi.org/10.3389/fpsyg.2021.661044
8. Hecht, L. K., Latzman, R. D., & Lilienfeld, S. O. (2017). The psychological treatment of psychopathy. *Evidence-Based Psychotherapy,* 271-298. https://doi.org/10.1002/9781119462996.ch11

17. Ideal 5: Find Power In Love and Connection

1. Zahn, R., Moll, J., Paiva, M., Garrido, G., Krueger, F., Huey, E. D., & Grafman, J. (2008). The neural basis of human social values: Evidence from functional MRI. *Cerebral Cortex, 19*(2), 276-283. https://doi.org/10.1093/cercor/bhn080
2. Chowdhury, M. R., & BA. (2021, November 27). *The neuroscience of gratitude and effects on the brain.* PositivePsychology.com. https://positivepsychology.com/neuroscience-of-gratitude/#neuroscience

3. Brown, J., & Wong, J. (2017, June 6). *How gratitude changes you and your brain*. Greater Good. https://greatergood.berkeley.edu/article/item/how_gratitude_changes_you_and_your_brain

4. Harvard Health. (2021, August 14). *Giving thanks can make you happier*. Harvard Health Publishing. https://www.health.harvard.edu/healthbeat/giving-thanks-can-make-you-happier

5. Brown, J., & Wong, J. (2017, June 6). *How gratitude changes you and your brain*. Greater Good. https://greatergood.berkeley.edu/article/item/how_gratitude_changes_you_and_your_brain

6. Harvard Health. (2021, August 14). *Giving thanks can make you happier*. Harvard Health Publishing. https://www.health.harvard.edu/healthbeat/giving-thanks-can-make-you-happier

18. Ideal 6: We, Not Me

1. Ghizoni, B. S. K. (2013, November 22). *Creation of the Bretton Woods System*. Federal Reserve History. https://www.federalreservehistory.org/essays/bretton-woods-created

2. Credit Suisse. (2021). *Annual reports*. https://www.credit-suisse.com/about-us/en/reports-research/annual-reports.html

19. Ideal 7: Believe in You, Believe In Us and Act With That Belief

1. Frankl, V. E. (1992). *Man's search for meaning: An introduction to logotherapy*. Beacon Press.

20. A New Life

1. Jewish Virtual Library. (n.d.). *Operation Ezra & Nehemia - The airlift of Iraqi Jews*. https://www.jewishvirtuallibrary.org/operation-ezra-and-nehemia-the-airlift-of-iraqi-jews

21. Fate Versus Destiny

1. Gutman, M., Zepeda, R., & Shapiro, E. (2018, June 5). *New details tie suspect to 6 killings within days in Arizona; targets connected to his divorce: Police*. ABC News. https://abcnews.go.com/US/4th-murder-arizona-linked-spree-began-killing-prominent/story?id=55626417

2. Emerald, D. (2015). *The power of ted: The empowerment dynamic.* Polaris Publishing.
3. Crab mentality can refer to a bucket of crabs not requiring a lid because their escape will be prevented by the other crabs who pull down each other, ensuring their collective demise.

Printed in the USA
CPSIA information can be obtained
at www.ICGtesting.com
LVHW091127211123
764443LV00031B/370/J